6-

CONFESSION
BRINGS
POSSESSION

D0878297

DON GOSSETT

Whitaker House

CONFESSION BRINGS POSSESSION

Don Gossett
P.O. Box 2
Blaine, WA 98230

ISBN: 0-88368-085-8
Printed in the United States of America
Copyright © 1979 by Don Gossett

Whitaker House
580 Pittsburgh Street
Springdale, PA 15144

4 5 6 7 8 9 10 11 12 13 / 05 04 03 02 01 00 99 98 97 96 95

CONFESSION
BRINGS
POSSESSION

CONTENTS

I'M SOLD ON BEING BOLD...

Chapter 1

BOLD AS A LION

When I was a young man, I experienced torment-ing fears in many areas of my life. I was reluctant, hesitant and fearful. Then the Lord called me into the ministry, and He miraculously transformed me from that fearful young man into an excited servant of God. For many years I lived free from fear in all of its forms. Then, in 1976, I experienced a crisis that, once again, brought me face-to-face with the difference between fearful, defeated living and the victory of bold Bible living.

For years there had been a mole on the side of my face. It was flat, about the size of my fingernail. When the mole began to change in color and size, it became really ugly in appearance. I'd comb my hair over my temple to hide its repulsiveness.

In February, 1976, my wife, Joyce, and I were preparing to leave for an overseas mission. We were having breakfast with our children when my son, Donnie, spoke up for all of them. "Dad, we're worried about that growth on the side of your head. Before you leave for this trip, we wish you would go to the doctor for an examination."

I consented to my children's request and that same afternoon was at a doctor's office in Surrey, British Columbia. The doctor carefully examined the growth and then asked me, in a serious tone of voice, "Reverend Gossett, how soon can you be ready for surgery?"

"Surgery?" I inquired. "I had no idea that you had such an action in mind."

The doctor responded, "It is imperative that you have surgery done as soon as possible. We must not delay."

I informed the doctor that we would be away until March first. He looked at his calendar and then scheduled my surgery for March 4th, 1976. He gravely informed me of the potential danger of the growth and that the surgery must not be postponed any later than that date.

When Joyce and I arrived overseas a few days later, I was battling with intense fears about the doctor's verdict. I was having what Harold Hill calls "an old-fashioned pity party." Why should this happen to me? Why should I be the "victim" of such a threatening situation?

One day I was standing and looking at myself in the mirror, lightly touching the growth and remembering the doctor's warning of its potential danger. Joyce saw me standing there and spoke out, "Somebody I know is having some real fears."

"Yes, that's right, honey," I admitted.

Joyce walked across the room to me, and I thought she was coming to share some words of tender, loving care. But you don't know my wife! When she was just a few feet from me, she looked at me sharply and said, "Shame on you!"

"Shame on me? Why did you say that?" I asked.

"You are the preacher that has written books on how to overcome fear; you have shared dozens of radio messages around the world on living free from fear all the days of your life. And now here you are—fearing."

"But, honey, this is for real . . ."

My wife boldly took action. She said to me, "Don, there are three things we must remember: 1) Surgery may be God's way for you in this situation. 2) Surgery may not be necessary, because the Lord may heal you in His own sovereignty. 3) Whatever happens, we must not give place to fear, because that would be giving place to the devil."

With those words, Joyce staunchly placed her hand upon my chest and began to rebuke the spirit of fear in the name of Jesus. That was one of the most remarkable liberations of my life! Suddenly the fear was all gone. It was like a fetter broken from my chest. I was free to breath deeply without any fear in my heart.

While the growth persisted and even became larger and uglier in the days ahead, I never feared it again. The Lord had liberated me totally from the tormenting spirits of fear, and I was free to praise God, confess His Word, and boldly anticipate the Lord's miracle for my life.

When we were flying home on March first, I reached up and accidently touched the growth. When I did so, about one-half of it fell out into my hand. Then during the night of March third, a tremendous miracle occurred. I rose early the next morning, felt my head, and was delighted to discover that where the rest of the growth had been, there was nothing there! I rushed to the mirror to examine it more closely and found that the growth was completely gone! Returning to my bed, I saw the remains of that growth scattered in my bedsheets.

Joyfully, I awakened Joyce and shared the wonderful news, "Honey, this is the day I'm scheduled for surgery...and there's nothing to '*surge*!'"

We rejoiced together at what the Lord had done! What a beautiful day March 4th was turning out to be.

At breakfast with Joyce and our son, Michael, we decided that I should keep the appointment for the scheduled surgery. I asked, a little curiously, "What am I going to say to the doctors today? Nothing like this has ever happened to me before."

Michael declared in a strong voice, "Dad, when you meet with those doctors today, just tell it like it is!"

When I arrived at the clinic for the scheduled surgery, I was met by a nurse. She led me to the room where I was to leave my clothes and wait until they were ready to perform the surgery. Just as we reached the room, I said, "Nurse, you may not have noticed, but I don't have the growth anymore."

She looked astonished, "You don't have the growth? What happened to it?"

With joy in my heart, I replied, "The Lord Jesus Christ has healed it completely!"

At the mention of the Lord healing me, the nurse looked rather frightened and quickly said, "I must get the doctors immediately." She scurried down the hall, away from the room.

In a few moments, the first doctor returned with my

medical chart in his hand. He studied the chart and then carefully examined my head. He repeated this process several times and then explained, "I better get the other doctor. He was involved in your case more than I was."

After a bit, the second doctor arrived. He was somewhat dubious about my account that the Lord had wrought a miracle for me. He eyed me curiously and asked, "What's this I hear about you working a wonder on yourself?"

"Doctor, *I* didn't do it. The *Lord* has done it, and I give Him the thanks and glory!"

For the next twenty minutes these physicians discussed the entire matter with me. I shared my experience exactly as it happened: How I had almost succumbed to the spirit of fear, how Joyce had prayed for me, and how the Lord had begun the healing process in the seventy-two hours just before the scheduled surgery. As I spoke, the doctors seemed to relax and were much more open in their attitudes.

After some time, the first doctor turned to the second one and asked, "Could this have been a work of nature?" But the other doctor only replied, "What *is* nature?"

As our discussion came to a close, both doctors pronounced my case dismissed. They acknowledged they had no part in the healing that had taken place. The Lord received all of the glory!

This miracle has stood the test for more than three years now. Never has any trace of that growth reappeared. I have thanked the Lord a hundred times . . . for the healing, for the victory over fear and for the continuing demonstration of the *power* of bold

Bible living.

It has been many years since God first led us to pioneer the message of *bold Bible living* on our radio broadcasts. It has meant a great deal in my own life, for it has been through this knowledge of God's Word that I have learned to live as the Bible says in Romans 8:37, as "More than conquerors through Christ who loved us."

What is *bold Bible living*? What does it mean?

First, bold Bible living means *living* with a capital "L." "He that hath the Son hath life" (1 John 5:12). When we receive Christ as Lord and Savior, God gives us LIFE abundant (John 10:10) and everlasting (John 3:16).

Second, we live by the *Bible*. Jesus taught us how to really live: "Man shall not live by bread alone, but by every word that proceedeth out of the mouth of God" (Matthew 4:4). My constant appeal in the ministry is to live by God's Word. This is Bible living.

Third, the Lord clearly led us to emphasize *bold* Bible living. In studying the Scriptures concerning bold Bible living, we discovered a tremendous promise of God.

Every one of us can be bold as a lion! Why? Because "The righteous are bold as a lion" (Proverbs 28:1).

Who are the righteous? Every born-again Christian! How? By faith in Jesus Christ! We have no righteousness of our own that can please God. But God made Jesus to become sin for us, that we might be made the righteousness of God in Christ (2 Corinthians 5:21).

Yes, we are the righteous of the Lord. And the

righteous are bold as a lion.

What does it mean to be "bold as a lion"? Primarily four things: (1) Confidence, (2) Courage, (3) Fearlessness, (4) Daring.

Confidence in Christ, not ourselves, that enables us to shout, "I can do all things through Christ which strengtheneth me" (Philippians 4:13).

Courage, the same Bible courage that characterized all of the righteous ones in the Bible. Consider such men and their deeds as Daniel, David, Elijah, Abraham, Joshua and Moses, to name only a few.

Fearlessness, the ability of God to enable us to live free from fear all our days. "For God hath not given us the spirit of fear; but of power, and of love, and of a sound mind" (2 Timothy 1:7).

Daring to act on the Word of God, to do what God says we can do.

These are four distinct qualities; yet they harmonize together. It is difficult to have one without possessing all four of them. The Word abounds with challenging truths that assure us that God gives these qualities and then expects us to use them. The Lord promises, "*Fear thou not;* for I am with thee: be not dismayed; for I am thy God..." (Isaiah 41:10). "For thus saith the Lord... in quietness and in *confidence* shall be your strength" (Isaiah 30:15). "Be strong and of a *good courage;* be *not afraid,* neither be thou dismayed: for the Lord thy God is with thee whithersoever thou goest" (Joshua 1:9).

Several passages from Joshua, chapter one, clearly reveal God's directive toward courageous living: to be strong and of good courage. This is bold living... being courageous under all adversities and learning that triumph goes to those who practice this truth. It is being able to say with David, "Though a host encamp against me, my heart shall not fear; though war arise against me, yet I will be *confident*!" (Psalm 27:3 *Revised Standard Version*).

In May of 1967 I was in Israel. When we came to that area where the Israelites were in array against the Philistines, my imagination vividly recalled the great event.

If a man ever displayed courage under fire, it was David in that hour. The whole army of Israel was terrified by the giant Goliath. No man could do battle with him. In fact, they were all cowards in his presence and in the face of his humiliating taunts against Israel. So overwhelming were the odds against the Israelite army that no man would even attempt to "save face" in that time of crisis.

We see David step out on that field of battle and challenge the giant who laughed at him. David was no coward. God had given him victories in the past against such formidable foes as a lion and a bear. This young man had courage...and courage was the needed quality here.

By the help of his God, David conquered the giant that day. What were his secrets? (1) He believed in his heart he could conquer Goliath, and he boldly declared the same. We, too, must confess our faith, confess the Scriptures, affirm boldly that what God has spoken is ours. (2) His courage was because of the name of the Lord. "I come to you in the name of the Lord," declared David. Our strength is in His name, also. "The name of the Lord is a strong tower: the righteous runneth into it, and is safe" (Proverbs 18:10).

An evangelist friend of mine, Velma Gardner, told me an amazing story one evening of a man who exhibited bold Bible living and courage in the Lord under very adverse circumstances. The story went like this:

"Years ago in a terrible blizzard, a Spirit-filled farmer was stranded many miles from nowhere. His car windshield was freezing over, and the wipers wouldn't work. The heater was nonexistent. He was in a desperate condition.

"This man told the Lord, 'Now, Lord, You know that I am many miles from my home. My wife is there without sufficient food. Lord, if You let me stay here, I'll freeze to death in a short time, and Mama will starve if I don't get home with the food.'

"Then the man did something daring. He said, 'Lord, You know that I can't see anything at all, so I'm going to start this car and commit it into Your hands to guide it.'

"This earnest Christian man started the car and drove it down those country roads, unable to see anything, but just turning the steering wheel as he was led by the Spirit of God. Mile after mile he drove along—by spiritual radar—turning curves and corners when he felt he should do so.

"Then suddenly the car came to a dead stop. The farmer looked down and saw that the ignition had been turned off. For a moment he was concerned and told the Lord so: 'Lord, You know this isn't my home. You have brought me thus far, but You can't let me stop here.' He looked out the window to survey his location when suddenly the express train went whizzing by. Had the car not stopped right when it

17

did, he would have been on the tracks when the train passed!

"The man bowed his head and said, 'Thank You, Lord. You knew more about the situation than I did.'

"The man turned on that ignition again, started the car, and later that afternoon arrived at his farm safe and sound!"

That is bold Bible living! Moving out boldly in the face of adverse circumstances, trusting the Lord to uphold you. "The people that do know their God shall be strong, and do exploits" (Daniel 11:32). I'm sold on being bold because those who are bold do exploits in the name of the Lord.

THE ALPHABET OF BOLD LIVING

The following is what I call my Alphabet of Bold Living. It covers many Scriptures that are our footholds for bold Bible living. Learn them and allow them to become a part of your heart. Then move out in bold exploits in God!

A— "All boldness to speak thy Word" (Acts 4:29).

B— "Bold in our God" (1 Thessalonians 2:2).

C— "Come boldly unto the throne of grace" (Hebrews 4:16).

D— "Draw nigh to God, and he will draw nigh to you" (James 4:8).

E— "Endued with power from on high" (Luke 24:49).

F— "Filled with the Holy Ghost, they spake the word of God with boldness" (Acts 4:31).

G— "Great is my boldness of speech" (2 Corinthians 7:4).

H— "Having boldness to enter into the holiest by the blood of Jesus" (Hebrews 10:19).

I— "I can do all things through Christ which strengtheneth me" (Philippians 4:13).

J— "Joy of the Lord is your strength" (Nehemiah 8:10).

K— "Know the truth, and the truth shall make you free" (John 8:32).

L— "Lo, he speaketh boldly" (John 7:26).

M—"Much bold in Christ" (Philemon 8).

N— "Nothing ashamed, but with all boldness, as always, so now also Christ shall be magnified in my body, whether it be by life, or by death" (Philippians 1:20).

O— "Obey God rather than men" (Acts 5:29).

P— "Paul spake boldly in the name of the Lord Jesus" (Acts 9:29).

Q— "Quench not the Spirit" (1 Thessalonians 5:19).

R— "Righteous are bold as a lion" (Proverbs 28:1).

S— "Saw the boldness of Peter and John . . . they took knowledge of them, that they had been with Jesus" (Acts 4:13).

T— "That we may have boldness in the day of judgment" (1 John 4:17).

U— "Utterance may be given unto me, that I may open my mouth boldly, to make known the mystery of the gospel . . . that I might speak boldly, as I ought to speak" (Ephesians 6:19-20).

V— "Violent take it by force" (Matthew 11:12).

W—"We may boldly say" (Hebrews 13:6).

X— "Wax bold" (Acts 13:46).

Y— "Ye are not your own . . . ye are bought with a price" (1 Corinthians 6:19-20).

Z— "Zealous of good works" (Titus 2:14).

Chapter 2

WHY WE CAN BE BOLD

The Lion of Judah

During World War II, one of the great battles was raging in northern France. Wave after wave of heavy artillery cracked through the atmosphere, one violent barrage after another. The noise of such explosive force was deafening. Suddenly, the guns ceased and there was silence! As the silence began to reign, the sweet music of a violin stole upon the air. One of the gunners had forgotten to turn his portable radio off.

The music was the B.B.C. studios from London sending waves of beautiful sound across the blood-stained fields of France. Indeed, it was as if heaven had broken forth on the scene of violence and death.

Actually, this is just what God did when He sent His Son to us. Amid the turmoil of a world under the devil's barrage of tension, darkness, fear, confusion, pain and clamor, God came to the earth in the person of the Lord Jesus Christ. Heaven broke forth with peace and assurance! The Sun of righteousness arose with healing in His wings (Malachi 4:2).

Jesus came at the lowest tide of human history. He

came at a time when the iron heel of Rome ruled most of the world, keeping men in bondage and fear. He came at a time when the religion of the One true God had lost its force and anointing, when it seemed the very doors of heaven were closed. He came at a time of widespread superstition and demon activity.

When Christ came to earth at such an hour, thousands turned their attention from Rome and Caesar and began looking to Jesus Christ.

Christ's bold ministry was the talk of the hour. The lame were walking, the blind were seeing, the dumb were speaking, the deaf were hearing, demons were being cast out, bread was being multiplied, water was being turned into wine, nature was being subdued, joy was leaping in the hearts of believers, angels were visiting men.

It was a bold ministry because Jesus recognized the devil's power in people's lives and moved boldly to cast him out. Even today, medical men and psychologists are working overtime combating the overwhelming power that brings doubt, fear, oppression, panic and mental illness. But it is still Jesus Christ who holds the key. He came to destroy the works of the devil, and He did it boldly! He did it as the "Lion of Judah" (Revelation 5:5).

Jesus was bold

They said of Jesus when He walked on the earth, "Lo, he speaketh boldly" (John 7:26). To speak boldly, one is first bold within, for Christ taught us, "Out of the abundance of the heart the mouth speaketh" (Matthew 12:34). Jesus was bold living personified!

Understanding that Bible boldness means confidence, courage, fearlessness and daring, we know indeed that Christ walked boldly throughout His ministry on earth. He was confident from whence He came and whither He was going. He was courageous to act and to declare it. He was fearless in the face of men's threats. He dared to make known His true identity.

Standing before the Jewish people one day as they were exalting their father, Abraham, Christ shocked them with His statement, "Before Abraham was, I am" (John 8:58).

Again and again Jesus declared Himself to be the great I AM. Consider these marvelous statements in the Gospel of John alone: "I am the bread of life" (John 6:35); "I am the light of the world" (John 9:5); "I am the door" (John 10:7); "I am the resurrection, and the life" (John 11:25).

And those who were close to Jesus, the Lion of Judah, had this same valuable quality of boldness. "Now when they saw the boldness of Peter and John . . . they took knowledge of them, that they had been with Jesus" (Acts 4:13).

Bold Bible living is not the unholy boldness so often demonstrated by the world. There were egotistical men in the Bible who had an unwholesome boldness. It was offensive and ugly.

Acts 5:36 tells of Theudas, "Boasting himself to be somebody" was "brought to nought." Real bold Bible living is not boasting. It savors not of self but of Christ.

Then we read of Simon the sorcerer, "giving out that himself was some great one" (Acts 8:9). But he was truly humbled by Peter's discernment, "Thy heart is not right in the sight of God. Repent therefore of this thy wickedness. . . . For I perceive that thou art in the gall of bitterness, and in the bond of iniquity" (Acts 8:21-23). It is still written in the Bible, "God resisteth the proud, but giveth grace unto the humble" (James 4:6).

Anyone who thinks that he is "some great one" is in the same deplorable condition as Simon whose "heart was not right in the sight of God."

There are people who are brash, loudmouthed, constantly seeking to call attention to themselves. They may consider themselves "bold as a lion." But that is not what we are talking about here. That is not the Jesus-quality of boldness.

Our foundation for bold living

The sole reason that we can experience boldness in our Christian walk is because Jesus was bold, and "as he is, so are we in this world" (1 John 4:17). The Word says that our boldness is entirely from "Christ Jesus our Lord: in whom we have boldness" (Ephesians 3:11-12). It is also through Christ's shed blood, "Having (possessing) boldness . . . by the blood of Jesus" (Hebrews 10:19).

Since Jesus, our Master, spoke and walked boldly, we, His followers, are to speak and walk boldly, too. When we know who we are in Christ, we will walk in confidence as He did. As we comprehend our rights in His name, we will courageously declare them and live by them. When we know what we can do in Christ, we can declare it fearlessly.

25

Remember who you are

The story is told that King Richard the Lion-hearted was so successful in defending England that his record was one of continual victory. One time, however, he was outmatched on the battlefield, as combined armies of other European powers were against him.

King Richard the Lion-hearted had a very loyal and trusted servant who always rode by his side in battle and was thrilled by the daring exploits of his king in conquest after conquest.

In this particular battle against the combined armies, the odds were so overwhelming that, for the first time in his brilliant career, King Richard the Lion-hearted sounded a retreat. This was an overwhelming sight for Richard's faithful servant, to see his own brave and noble king leading a retreat.

As the servant ran his horse with King Richard, he remembered battle after battle where the king had so gallantly led the English army to astonishing victory. Now it was a sad, dismal, frustrating defeat.

To conceive of King Richard the Lion-hearted being defeated was more than the trusted servant could endure. So, the story is told, the servant raced his horse right next to the king and shouted in his ear, "King Richard, *remember who you are!*"

These words penetrated the king's heart, and suddenly he gave the command to his bugler to sound a halt to the retreat. Then, in a bit of bold strategy, the command was given "to advance and conquer."

According to history, this was the experience that turned back the combined armies that day...when King Richard the Lion-hearted suddenly was compelled to remember who he was ... a mighty conqueror, a king who had never known or accepted defeat. This is the secret of bold Bible living: *Remember Who You Are!* Learn to respect what God has placed within you. Read the Bible to learn who you are in Christ.

Who are we in Christ?

One of my favorite sayings is this one: When you were born again, you were not born to be defeated; you were born to conquer. I believe that because Romans 8:37 tells us, "Nay, in all these things we are more than conquerors through him who loved us."

We are more than conquerors! We are children of God, dear to Him, and joint-heirs with Christ. We have great riches in Jesus! We are heirs of all things. We are who God made us to be.

We are a branch of the living vine, for Jesus said, "I am the vine, ye are the branches" (John 15:5). We are the temple of the living God, for the Bible says, "Ye are the temple of the living God; as God hath said, I will dwell in them, and walk in them; and I will be their God, and they shall be my people" (2 Corinthians 6:16).

What can we do in Christ?

We can do all things, whatsoever needs to be accomplished. The Lord gives us the ability to do all He commands of us so that we can say with Paul, "I can do all things through Christ which strengtheneth me" (Philippians 4:13).

What do we have in Christ?

We have life, we have light, we have power, we have peace, we have provision for our needs, we have all things that pertain to life and godliness (2 Peter 1:3).

Yes, to be a Christian is more than just being a forgiven sinner. We are heirs of God and joint-heirs with Christ Jesus; we are linked with God by the new birth; and we are partakers of His very nature. No wonder we can sing and shout and be glad today, when we know what it really means to be a child of God!

Just remember who you are right in the midst of your battles. Don't accept defeat. Defeat may come and stare you right in the face. Refuse to accept it!

Boldly sound a halt to your retreat. Sound the new note of advance and conquer. Yes, you are a conqueror through Christ who indwells your life!

Therefore be bold

Because of who we are in Christ, there is abundant reason for living boldly, for being confident, courageous and daring. What is there to be gained by being fearful, timid, or inferior? "Be bold and great forces will come to your aid," said a wise man in times past. On our *Bold Bible Living* broadcasts, we do not theorize vaguely about bold living. But we, like Paul of New Testament times, "use great plainness of speech." We use the Word of God in clear and ringing challenge: Therefore be bold! In Christ you have boldness, therefore use it! "Having therefore, brethren, boldness to enter the holiest by the blood of Jesus" (Hebrews 10:19).

The Bible records in Acts 4:29, 31, "Lord ... grant unto thy servants, that with all boldness they may speak thy word.... and they were all filled with the Holy Ghost, and they spake the word of God with boldness."

The element of boldness in the Christian is no accident. Nor is it something to be worked up by self-effort. It is an inherent part of the Christian. Christ has inoculated us with this daring, courageous quality— therefore be bold in being bold!

Use what Christ has put in you. There is no room in the Christian life for the conventional, shy, barely-able-to-keep-head-above-water existence that some believe represents the Christian. Read the Word of God, especially the four Gospels and the book of Acts, and you will see that Christ's unceasing appeal to His disciples was to translate the spiritual into daring action.

Now, in the rest of this book, we are going to challenge you to experience this bold Bible living in every area of your lives. How to be bold in your family life, in the confession of God's Word, in your prayers, in your finances, in your job, in your witnessing and in your praise. This was Jesus' message nearly two thousand years ago, and it has not changed today!

Therefore be bold!

I'M SOLD ON BEING BOLD

I want to tell you why I'm sold on being bold as a Christian. "The righteous are bold as a lion" (Proverbs 28:1). You and I are righteous through Christ, and God expects the righteous to be bold as a lion!

I'm sold *because Jesus was bold.* "Lo, he speaketh boldly" (John 7:26). To be bold means to be confident, courageous, fearless and daring. Jesus was our example in all of these qualities.

I'm sold *because boldness is indeed a Jesus-like quality.* When they saw the boldness of Peter and John ... they took knowledge of them, that they had been with Jesus" (Acts 4:13).

I'm sold *because the desire for boldness was the passion of the early Christians.* They were filled with the Holy Spirit, they had been entrusted to use the name of Jesus, they had the Word of God. But when they prayed, here was their request: "Lord, ... grant unto thy servants, that with ALL BOLDNESS we may speak thy word" (Acts 4:29).

I'm sold *because the Holy Ghost produces this holy boldness.* Remember, of the early Christians we read, "They were all filled with the Holy Ghost, and they spake the word of God with boldness" (Acts 4:31). There are three Bible sins against the Holy Spirit that Christians can commit: We can resist the Spirit, quench the Spirit or grieve the Spirit. If we do not, but rather yield to the Spirit, He will produce boldness in us.

I'm sold *because of the power of Jesus' name*. Acts 9:27 and 29 tells how Paul spoke boldly in the name of Jesus. When we know that God has given Jesus the name above all names (Philippians 2:9), and that Jesus has entrusted to us the use of His mighty name, we will be bold to speak in His name against sickness, demons, fears, lack, and financial needs.

I'm sold *because of the dynamic results of bold action*. Acts 13:46 declares that Paul and Barnabas "waxed bold." To wax bold is bold action. David not only spoke boldly when he was confronted with the giant Goliath, but he "waxed bold" in action. Jesus warned that in the end-times "the love of many shall wax cold." Make it your testimony, "My love for Christ is waxing bold, not cold."

I'm sold *because speaking the Word boldly produces signs and wonders*. Acts 14:3, "Long time therefore abode they speaking boldly in the Lord, which gave testimony unto the word of his grace, and granted signs and wonders to be done by their hands." Peter and John spoke boldly at the beautiful gate, and the lame man was miraculously healed! Philip was bold in going to wicked Samaria, and the Lord worked mightily through him in great miracles!

31

I AM BLEST WITH HEAVEN'S BEST...

Chapter 3

MAN TO MAN

Some years ago I returned home from evangelistic travels to discover lions in my home!

My wife had little miniature lions of every size and shape and made out of many different materials strategically placed in various parts of our home.

"What is the meaning of these little lions?" I asked her.

Joyce smiled, "Honey, I appreciate what the Lord has done for you so much since you have begun to live up to your rights in Jesus, that I don't want you to forget *who you are.*"

She was referring, of course, to the study of the Bible that we had made together, when Proverbs 28:1 opened to us: "The wicked flee when no man pursueth: but the righteous are bold as a lion."

Since that day, Joyce has continued to purchase little lions in our travels and friends have added to the collection. Through the years, they have served as a constant reminder that we have made a commitment in Jesus Christ to walk in bold Bible living.

However, those little lions in my house said

something else very crucial to me that day, something that has gained in importance over the years, and that is: *bold Bible living must begin in the home*!

God plans for our homes to be a refuge from the storms, pressures and disappointments of life. God never planned that our homes should be jeopardized by selfishness, endangered by bad tempers, nor set at hazard by spirits of jealousy, sulkiness or boredom.

Your home in Christ should be a haven, your stronghold spiritually, mentally and physically. It should provide an alternative to the evil forces of Satan; the divorce, rebellion, unhappiness and pain that is destroying families throughout the world.

Your home may not be expensive, but it is your castle, your ark of happiness, shutting out sin, degradation and the filth of the world.

As Christians, we need to have the courage and boldness in our homes to do things God's way in the face of pressures from the world to do it Satan's way. We know by God's Word that we have the right to have sound, happy marriages; we have the right to have husbands or wives that love and enjoy us; we have the right to expect children that obey and honor us. However, we must make a bold decision to follow the pattern of God's Word in order to obtain these things. Every mail-call that comes to me speaks of crumbling marriages and homes that are on the quicksand of destruction. But God's Word can and will escort us into bold Bible living that will safeguard our homes.

With so many marriages on a shaky foundation, tottering on a pillar of self-love, I believe that I must speak plainly to my fellow Christian brothers.

If I understand the Bible correctly, God requires a

great deal of us men whom He has chosen to be the heads of our households. "For the husband is the head of the wife, even as Christ is the head of the church . . ." (Ephesians 5:23). Also, an overseer (or any man who longs to truly serve God) must be one who manages his own household well (1 Timothy 3:2, 4). But sadly, many men in the kingdom of God do not know how to take a bold stand as spiritual and practical leaders in the home. It is an area that I cannot give enough emphasis to in an age when Satan is attempting to destroy the foundation of all human relationships: the family.

A bold word for husbands

"For the husband is the head of the wife, even as Christ is the head of the church. . . . Husbands, love your wives, even as Christ also loved the church, and gave himself for it. . . . So ought men to love their wives as their own bodies. . . . For this cause shall a man leave his mother and father, and shall be joined unto his wife, and they two shall be one flesh" (Ephesians 5:23, 25, 28, 31).

These verses reveal two very important parts of our role as Christian men. First, we are to be the heads of our families, the leaders of our homes. Then, just as importantly, we are to love our wives as much as Jesus Christ Himself loved the church. A love as strong as the one that Christ had for us as He hung on the cross! It should be stronger than a husband's love for his parents, his children, or anyone else, except the Lord. The husband should see to it that it is so, for it has been commanded by the Word of God.

Many husbands have created an unstable home

condition because of being vulnerable at this point: Failure to love their wives more dearly than anyone or anything else on earth. I am especially aware of the mistakes some husbands make in crushing their wives because I grew up with a very strong-willed, dominant father. He caused my mother a lot of heartache because of his infidelity and his selfish drunkeness. Praise the Lord, by the time I was eighteen years old, my father came to know Jesus Christ as Lord. But through the early years, I saw the utter dominance he held over my mother and the lack of love he showed her, and I resolved to be the opposite of my Dad's early years and to follow the Lord's commandments to love my wife.

How can we apply this bold commandment to love our wives as Christ loved the church?

I believe in this day of male chauvinism and woman's liberation that it takes a strong Christian man to love his wife in spite of all that the world has to say against it. And it can only be done with the Jesus-kind of love.

My wife and I made a thorough study of a book by E. W. Kenyon entitled *The New Kind Of Love* which helped us a great deal and convinced us that the characteristics of Jesus' love is the real answer for a bold living Christian home.

Dr. Kenyon points out that the Jesus-kind of love is only possible to those who have experienced the new birth. When Jesus comes to dwell in our hearts by the Holy Spirit, He brings the very nature of God into us. Since God is love (1 John 4:8), when He comes to live in our hearts, His love becomes a part of us. The Bible says, "The love of God is shed abroad in our hearts by the Holy Spirit" (Romans 5:5).

38

The Jesus-kind of love is one that sacrifices and gives for those He loves. Jesus was a Man who walked this earth in love, showing compassion to those with needs, denying Himself so that He could minister life to those around Him. Jesus loved us by doing real things. He loved the sick, so He reached out and healed them. He loved us all so much that He went to the cross and died for us. It is this same kind of love that He expects us to have for our wives and for each other today. Remember the Bible says, "Husbands, love your wives as Christ loved the church, and *gave himself for it.*"

Dr. Kenyon goes on to say of the Jesus-kind of love, "This love is a home builder and a home preserver. This is God's method of protecting marriage. When this kind of love gains the ascendency in the hearts of husbands (and wives), no other law is necessary to preserve the home.... With this kind of love, divorce will never take place in the Jesus home."

Surrounded by the frequent and easy divorces of today, that is not a claim to pass over lightly! It is one that Joyce and I have found in our own lives and in counseling others to be 100% true. The Jesus-kind of love is the answer!

The Bible position is straightforward that the husband is the head of the wife, but that doesn't mean an egocentric possessiveness. It means leadership with real empathy, with caring and sharing that is thoroughly tempered by love.

Another primary cause for the breakdown of so many homes in our day, even Christian ones, is the increase of infidelity, permissive sex or "wife-swapping." It is time for Christians to take a bold

Bible stand against these wiles of Satan in their own homes.

Frequently, I counsel with wives as well as husbands who are in the midst of a marriage breaking up because of unfaithfulness to the marriage vows. Next to the pure motivation of loving my wife as Christ loved the church, I have discovered that true reverence and fear of the Lord are the greatest preventatives to playing the fool and committing adultery as a husband. Hebrews 13:4 speaks so plainly, "Marriage is honorable in all, and the bed undefiled: but whoremongers and adulterers God will judge." I do not know what this special judgement of God that comes upon adulterers may be, but I fear the Lord too much to subject myself to the possibility of becoming a candidate for it. I have witnessed firsthand the judgement of God that has come upon many men, and I do not desire it for myself.

My wife and I were well-acquainted with a couple who were also in the Lord's work. We had many times of fellowship together and enjoyed each other's company. In order to share their story, I will call them Larry and Jean.

One evening several years ago, Larry was entertained by a businessman and his wife in another city. The businessman's wife was about twenty years younger than Larry and was a very attractive woman. As often as she could after that first evening, this woman would get together with my minister friend for counsel, special times of prayer, dinners, or what have you. For a long time the situation seemed to be well-in-hand as the businessman was either along or else was identified with the times of fellowship. But slowly the woman arranged to see Larry more and more often by herself. Her contact with him began to make inroads upon his life. Larry was far too dedicated to the Gospel to have been caught off-guard in one sweep, but like water dripping on sand, little by little, the woman's contacts made their impact.

Then came the night when, quite by surprise, I met my friend and this woman alone in a car. My heart sank. I knew that a total collapse of Larry's morals and marriage were imminent.

I cannot piece together all that happened in the months that followed, but there were witnesses who knew of the complete deterioration of this man's marriage and ministry because of his adulterous relationship.

One day Joyce and I received an urgent phone call from Larry's wife, Jean. She told us that her husband had asked her for a divorce, that he loved this other woman and was going to marry her. Larry would be home for a final dinner with his family, and then would proceed with the divorce. Heartbroken, Jean asked us to join the family for this dinner. With tears she begged us to come, praying that God, by His mercy, would undertake and touch Larry's heart and that there would be a reconciliation of the marriage. She was willing to forgive her husband for his unfaithfulness because she loved him and because she knew it would be God's will for all of them.

It was with deeply mixed emotions we sat around the dinner table at Larry's home that night. Except for the oldest daughter, the children were not aware that this was to be their last meal together as a family. Because Larry had been away a fair amount, the children were unusually happy to have him there. We prayerfully ate that meal with the family, emotionally moved in our hearts by this precious wife and her sorrow-stricken countenance. Larry pretended that everything was all right, but he too was shaky through the whole dinner.

After the meal, we all went into the living room. Larry's only son, a seven-year-old boy, insisted on sitting on his dad's knee. Repeatedly, the boy would throw his arms around his dad's neck and squeeze him tight. The Holy Spirit used the love and devotion of that little boy to break Larry's heart. As we all sat there watching, suddenly Larry jumped up and rushed to the adjoining bedroom where he threw himself across the bed and cried his eyes out.

How glad I am to report: that was the beginning of the salvation of their marriage. Larry truly repented of his sins to God and then with humility asked his wife's forgiveness. Restoration had begun. While it took them a little time to complete that restoration, by the power of the Holy Spirit it was done. A marriage was saved. A home was kept together. And this home has continued to remain intact and to grow in bold Christian living for all the years since then. Praise the Lord!

Husbands! Look out, sir, that woman is God's beacon in your life. There is the one and only woman that has entrusted all to you. She even took your name. Before marriage you promised fine, bright, beautiful expectations in her heart . . . live up to them!

So many husbands (even Christian ones!) are unfair and inconsiderate to their wives, taking everything for granted, forgetting even the common courtesy to be polite and appreciative. Thanking their wives for something as simple as cooking their favorite meal, or any other job that was done in love, is often not considered. Remember, men, your wives are joint-heirs to the Kingdom of God along with you.

First Peter 3:7 says, "Likewise, ye husbands, dwell with them (your wives) *according to knowledge*, giving honor unto the wife, as unto the weaker vessel, and as being heirs together of the grace of life; that your prayers be not hindered."

Your wife needs understanding, respect and the help of her husband. The Bible says that she is the weaker vessel, so you should be her major source of encouragement in the problems and annoyances that come upon her due to Satan's wiles, the world, the children, or the everyday tensions of life. If you do not dwell with her in the knowledge of her needs, your prayers actually will not reach the throne of God!

When the Bible tells husbands to dwell with their wives in all knowledge, I believe that extends from the most crucial times down to the daily joys and ways of loving that will bless our wives.

Since I have been called by the Lord to serve as an evangelist, it has been necessary for me to be apart from my wife a total of thousands of days and nights in our years together. Now there is one very practical way that I have loved my wife through all of that traveling. I always made it a love practice to keep in touch with Joyce as much as possible. In the early years when money was a particular hardship, I would write her at least one letter a day from wherever I was just to keep in touch with her and to let her know how much I love her. It also made her feel a very vital part of my ministry in places where she could not accompany me. In more recent years, since the Lord has blessed us with a global ministry, when I have to be away from my wife overseas I call her as often as possible. We do not abuse the time and money needed for these calls. But I believe with all my heart that it is a vital part of my ministry as head of my household and a godly husband to see to it that my wife is cared for and loved. What good does it do if I am out ministering the Gospel and my wife is at home struggling with responsibilities that we need to handle together? How well can I represent the Lord Jesus I serve if I am disobeying His very clear commandment to love my wife and dwell with her in all knowledge?

What about you, husband? Does your wife like to have little surprises every once in a while? Dwell with her in all knowledge and bring her home a surprise. Does she like to go out to dinner at certain times of the year? Does she like flowers or special help with the children? Show her some love and honor as your joint-heir in Jesus Christ and treat her to those times. It is a very important part of your ministry within the home. If your home expresses the love of Jesus in all of these ways, your witness to the outside world—a world lost and dying without Jesus Christ—will be attracted to that love you have together.

In these days of increasing family turmoil, I am boldly sounding the alarm, for we husbands hold the key to home harmony and having God's best, even for accomplishing His will upon the earth through dedicated Christian families. In fact, you can never truly know God's best in every area of your life and ministry as long as the home condition is wrong.

According to Paul's instructions in the first epistle to Timothy, a man who does not have his house in order cannot even have the ministry of bishop, overseer or deacon. There is no reason why the same admonition to have your house in order before all other ministry should not be applicable to every man in the Body of Christ, whether he has a ministry as an overseer, is an evangelist or serves the Lord in a secular position.

Men, servants of Christ, don't succumb to Satan's wiles to either be an unbearable tyrant in your home or just a lazy man giving your authority over to your wife. Either position is unscriptural and out of the will of God.

Instead, make a bold stand for Christ. Serve the Lord as a strong Christian leader in your home. Love your wives in the midst of a perverse generation that knows little of the meaning of the Jesus-kind of love! Stand up for bold Bible living in your home. Consecrate it to God!

NO ROOM FOR COMPROMISE

I want to speak out to husbands for dedicated Christian living. There is no room for compromise with worldliness or carnal living. I love the crisp Bible terms: holiness, purity, sanctification, righteousness, dedication. It is especially important for the husband who stands as the head of his household to see that these are values his entire family honors. Here are fifteen reasons why your life will be unusually blessed as you seek God's honor.

1. "Godliness is profitable unto all things, having promise of the life that now is, and of that which is to come" (1 Timothy 4:8).

2. "Be not conformed to this world: but be ye transformed by the renewing of your mind, that you may prove what is that good, and acceptable, and perfect will of God" (Romans 12:2).

3. "The peace of God, which passeth all understanding, shall keep your hearts and minds through Christ Jesus" (Philippians 4:7).

4. "Draw nigh to God, and he will draw nigh to you. Cleanse your hands, ye sinners; and purify your hearts, ye double-minded" (James 4:8).

5. "Righteousness shall go before Him; and shall set us in the way of His steps" (Psalm 85:13).

6. "He that followeth after righteousness and mercy findeth life, righteousness, and honor" (Proverbs 21:21).

7. "Thus saith the Lord, Stand ye in the ways, and see, and ask for the old paths, where is the good way, and walk therein, and ye shall find rest for your souls" (Jeremiah 6:16).

8. "To him that soweth righteousness shall be a sure reward" (Proverbs 11:18).

9. "Thou, Lord, wilt bless the righteous; with favor wilt thou compass him as with a shield" (Psalm 5:12).

10. "A highway shall be there, and a way, and it shall be called The way of holiness" (Isaiah 35:8).

11. "I am come a light into the world, that whosoever believeth on me should not abide in darkness" (John 12:46).

12. "Lord, who shall abide in thy tabernacle? Who shall dwell in thy holy hill? He that walketh uprightly, and worketh righteousness, and speaketh the truth in his heart"

(Psalm 15:1-2).

13. "For the righteous Lord loveth righteous-
    ness; his countenance doth behold the
    upright" (Psalm 11:7).

14. "For the eyes of the Lord run to and fro
    throughout the whole earth, to show
    himself strong in the behalf of them whose
    heart is perfect toward him" (2 Chronicles
    16:9).

15. "If our heart condemn us not, then have we
    confidence toward God" (1 John 3:21).

Summary: You will be a God-pleasing Christian
husband and spiritual leader in your home as you
live by these passages and enter into the fulfillment of them!

Chapter 4

TRAIN UP A CHILD

Are men lousy fathers?

Some time ago, *Reader's Digest* carried an article entitled "Are Men Lousy Fathers?" To discover how much time fathers and sons spent together, 300 seventh and eighth grade boys kept accurate records for a two-week period. The average time that father and son had alone together for an entire week was seven-and-a-half minutes!

Too many dads, even Christian ones, are like guests in their own home, nearly as strangers to their children. Sir, you may work to provide for your family, but do you truly live with them? Do you provide the leadership and guidance that they need to receive from you? Oh, that we fathers would only realize the brief time we have with our children! It's a sad thing when some men forlornly note in their later years, as did one president of a well-known college. "If I only had it to do all over again, I certainly would have given more time and attention to my five sons when they were growing up."

When David Wilkerson, youth leader and author of

The Cross and The Switchblade, was in Vancouver, I had a visit with him one afternoon in his hotel room.

Brother Wilkerson said very solemnly to me, "Among the greatest tragedies I've known have been the missionaries and ministers who have gone out to save the whole world but have lost their own children!"

This is indeed a tragedy!

King David was a tremendous man as God's anointed and a leader. But as a father, David was almost a total failure. What grief and anguish he relates through the pages of Scripture concerning his bitter disappointments in his own sons.

Eli, priest of God, the man chosen to teach the prophet Samuel the things of the Lord, was shamed for his place as a father. He received God's stern rebuke and disapproval because of his failure to correct his sons when they sinned and indulged in ungodly living. Eli's entire household suffered shame, and his two sons and Eli himself died on the same day because of Eli's failure to be a godly father (1 Samuel 2:12-4:18). Surely this is no light matter in the eyes of the Lord!

When my own five children were small and readily kept in order by Joyce and me, I pondered, "Is it possible my children will rebel against our authority? Will they forsake the Lord and His teachings?"

This became one of my goals of top priority—to succeed as a father. As the children grew up, I loved to play with them; we had ball games together. We enjoyed each other's company (and still do). And we have always liked to work together.

As their father, I prayed much for my five children,

"Lord, keep them from harm and danger, from disease and affliction. May they grow up to love You, Lord, with all their hearts."

To me, it would seem a mockery to go out and try to "save the world" and lose my own children.

In view of the repeated catastrophes shared with me by godly ministers who have lost their children to the world, I needed to secure a bold foundation of truth that would enable me to raise my five children to love and serve the Lord Jesus Christ.

As with any area of bold Bible living, the Bible became my instruction manual on how to have God's complete best.

Joshua, leader of Israel long ago, was a powerful example. He made a bold stand that has helped to lay a foundation for my position as a Christian father. When faced with the temptation of the world and all that the false gods of worldly living had to offer, Joshua boldly affirmed, "As for me and my house, *we will serve the Lord*" (Joshua 24:15).

It is absolutely the responsibility of the head of the household to make that same confession, "As for me and my *wife*, we will serve the Lord"; "As for me and my *sons*, we will serve the Lord"; "As for me and my *daughters*, we will serve the Lord!" No exception, not one prodigal in the family. No black sheep, nothing of that nature. Just 100% total salvation for the whole family. It's a confession of faith based on Acts 16:31, "Believe on the Lord Jesus Christ, and thou shalt be saved, and thy house." And it's a determination in Christ, "As for me and my house, *we will serve the Lord!*"

I know the story of one man who took this scripture

51

and responsibility very seriously. For years, hanging just over his dining room table was a beautiful plaque with the scripture motto, "As for me and my house, we will serve the Lord." This man had one son who had turned his back on God, so he called that young man in for a private consultation one day, and said:

"Son, I'm very grieved. We've had that motto for the last twenty years of our marriage and the raising of this family. Now, I'm going to take it down."

"But why, Dad?" his son questioned, puzzled.

"Because I'm not going to live a lie," his father answered determinedly. "It's not true anymore. My house is no longer serving the Lord, and because of your ways we're going to have to take it down. I refuse to have that up there when you are not a fulfillment of it."

That sincere determination to stand strong in the Word of God so touched the boy's heart that it caused him to see the folly of his ways. A short time later, he turned back to serving the Lord!

I would to God that every father, every husband reading these lines would make this your bold stand, "As for me and my house, *we will serve the Lord*!"

It was C. H. Spurgeon who once said, "Show me a loving husband, a worthy wife and good children, and no pair of horses that ever flew along the road could take me in a year where I would see a more pleasing sight. Home is the grandest of all institutions." I heartily agree.

As I continued to study the Word and search for other strong examples of godly fathers in the Bible, I came across the testimony of Abraham. In the Old

Testament, Abraham stands out as one of the grandest men in history. Have you ever considered why God could so confide in Abraham and commit sacred trusts to him? Genesis 18:19 gives God's answer: "For I know him (Abraham), *that he will command his children and his household after him,* and they shall keep the way of the Lord, to do justice and judgment."

God knew that Abraham could train up and control his children. It has been my heart's desire to follow after Abraham's example in the training up of my own children.

For many years I have studied this subject: How to boldly train your children to be clean, honorable, dedicated Christians. The book of Proverbs gives us clear admonition on how to be parents to our children in a way that will produce real Christian character.

"Train up a child in the way he should go: and when he is old, he will not depart from it" (Proverbs 22:6).

Training a child demands love, discipline, guidance and careful instruction. But more than that it requires example. To the children a father is a flesh-and-blood example of manhood. I believe a father's job is to teach his sons to become men, and it is a father's responsibility to show his daughers what a true Christian man should be.

Besides the necessity of showing forth a good example to our children, we are also to train them up through godly discipline. The Bible says, "He who spares his rod hates his son, but he who loves him disciplines him diligently" (Proverbs 13:24 *New American Standard*). And "Foolishness is bound in the heart of a child; but the rod of correction shall drive it far from him'' (Proverbs 22:15).

It is necessary to set out to diligently discipline our children when they have disobeyed us. It is a command of God and will only bring good to their lives.

"Correct thy son, and he shall give thee rest; yea, he shall give delight unto thy soul'' (Proverbs 29:17).

When my son, Donnie, was about four years old, we were in a department store together where he spotted some little guns that fascinated him. He asked me if I would please buy them, but because I knew he had enough toys at home, I said no.

After we left the store and walked just a short way, I noticed something sticking out from under his shirt. I asked him what it was, and he answered slowly, "It's the guns I wanted, Daddy.''

Immediately, I dealt with the situation, explained to Donnie it was wrong, and then spanked him for his disobedience. He returned the two little guns to the store manager.

Then, four years later, a similar situation occurred. Donnie picked something up in a store even though he had the money to pay for it. He thought it was so convenient and well-hidden in the back of the room. He never thought anyone would see him. However, the saleswoman did see him, and it wasn't long before I got a call at my office about my son's misdeed.

At first, I was a little frightened. Would Donnie always be tempted by these kinds of situations? Would my son become a thief? But I knew the Word said that the rod of correction would drive this foolishness from his heart (Proverbs 22:15), so I decided to stand on the Word.

Now, it makes no difference whether you are a minister of the Gospel or not. These things can and need to be dealt with according to God's Word. I explained to Donnie how it is scripturally wrong to steal and to disobey. Then, I disciplined him by a good sound spanking. Well, praise the Lord, it never happened again! As a matter of fact, we saw so many blessed things come from Donnie in the future that it confirmed God's Word that a disciplined child would truly delight his parents' soul (Proverbs 29:17).

One of my fondest memories from Donnie's childhood was a few years after this incident. One night as Joyce was kissing all of the children goodnight, Donnie asked her to pray for a little boy at school. He told her what had happened that day.

"Mommy, there is a little boy who is just in the first grade this year (Donnie was in the sixth), who was taking his school things home in a paper bag. On the school bus as we were going home, the little boy's bag broke and all of his crayons, pencils and papers began spilling out onto the bus floor and rolling under the seats. He kept trying to pick them up, but they kept slipping from his hands. The older boys were laughing at him and making fun and even hiding some of his things from him."

Then Donnie said, "Mommy, I looked at this little boy's face, and two big tears were rolling down his cheeks as he was trying to get all of his things together. And the older boys laughed at him more because of his tears."

"What did you do, Donnie?" my wife asked quietly.

He burst into tears and said, "Mommy, I got down on my knees and helped him pick up his things, and then I helped him off the bus when we got to his home."

So, as Donnie was crying about his young school friend, Joyce quietly prayed for the little boy and also thanked God for giving our Donnie such a tender, loving heart.

What a blessing it is for parents to see their efforts to raise their children in the admonition of the Lord bring such fruit, just as the Lord promised in His Word!

I would like to interject one very important word here before going on. I sincerely believe that a child should only be spanked out of a motive of love and the desire to give godly correction. Children shouldn't be spanked for reasons that have nothing to do with the child. Some parents just grab their children and begin beating on them to take out their own frustrations. The Bible says that a child is to be disciplined for his *own good* that he may grow up in the love and ways of the Lord, not to release tension in a parent that should really be released through a Spirit-filled relationship to Jesus Christ as Lord.

The Bible says, "Fathers, do not irritate and provoke your children to anger—do not exasperate them to resentment—but rear them [tenderly] in the training and discipline and the counsel and admonition of the Lord" (Ephesians 6:4 *The Amplified Bible*). We must seek to administer discipline to our children tenderly and in love.

What will be the result if correction is withheld? "The rod and reproof give wisdom: *but a child left to himself bringest his mother shame*" (Proverbs 29:15). There is even danger in delaying correction too long.

"Chasten thy son while there is hope, and let not thy soul spare for his crying" (Proverbs 19:18).

It is a solemn business to be entrusted by God to be a father, to be the spiritual leaders of our homes! To stand boldly before the world and, as Abraham, to command our children and our household after us!

When I realized the awesome burden of my responsibility, I went directly to the Lord in prayer, seeking Him as my help and my strength. I wondered how I would ever be able to complete my godly role as a father without losing my children to the world. The Lord spoke to me clearly from the Scriptures, "I can do all things through Christ which strengtheneth me" (Philippians 4:13). I can do *all* things through Christ! *All* things!

This became my bold declaration: "I can do all things through Christ which strengtheneth me. I *can* succeed as a father. I *can* train my children up to love the Lord. I *can* do it through Christ!"

Oh, the joy that I experienced in knowing that I had so much from the Scriptures to stand on. The testimonies of Joshua and Abraham, the words of direction and promise from the book of Proverbs, and now the firm assurance from God that *I can do it all through Christ!*

Admittedly, there have been problems. God gave us two sons and three daughters . . . not angels. There has been temporary rebellion and waywardness. But as quickly as these situations arose, through Christ's strength we coped with them.

As the spiritual leader of my home, I learned to take a bold stand for God and against Satan for the total salvation of our children, spiritually, mentally, emotionally and physically. With my wife by my side in agreement, we stood boldly in Christ in overcoming all of the satanic forces designed for our children's destruction and downfall.

Certainly, we made some mistakes along the way. But we learned how to raise our children by trusting in God and the promises of His Word that we can do all things through Christ!

At the present hour I can share this report: Praise the Lord, our children—all grown now—love the Lord in sincerity. The boys, Michael and Donnie, are serving the Lord in music. Judy is singing with Reba Rambo, the beautiful Gospel singer. Jeanne Michele works in our offices, and young Marisa is presently attending Bible college.

Thankfully, my children have a high respect for their parents. We enjoy a good relationship—in Christ.

It's no "feather-in-our-caps." We don't live under a "lucky star." We can do all things through Christ, including raising our children to be strong Christians. Fathers, take a bold stand in Jesus! You can do it through His strength!

BOLD FATHER'S GUIDE

Fathers, the following are some signposts to success as God's man in your home.

1. Be a glad dad in the Lord. What a testimony real joy is to your children.

2. Spend time with your children! Don't be like the seven-and-a-half-minutes-a-week fathers from *Reader's Digest*. Do things with your children that they enjoy and that will mean something to them, even if it takes some of your own scarce free time.

3. Teach your children to memorize Bible verses and then to be doers of the verses that they learn. How permanent a foundation for good and blessing when they hide God's Word within their hearts. Saturating the lives of our children with God's Word has been our constant pursuit ever since they were babies.

4. Among the sweetest times you can have with your children is in family worship. I have always endeavored to make that time very important. It should never be monotonous, dull or tedious, which is a treason to true worship. Rather, it should be so pleasant as to be looked forward to with gladness, even by the youngest children.

5. Lead your children into the Spirit-filled life. Urge them to keep filled with the Holy Spirit, then the base things of the world cannot crowd in and get a hold.

6. Prepare your children to live free from fear all their days by instilling the sure words of God: "God hath not given us the spirit of fear; but of power, and of love, and of a sound mind" (2 Timothy 1:7).

7. Help your children overcome any inferiority complex by the joyful awareness that "I live; yet not I, but Christ liveth in me" (Galatians 2:20).

8. Instruct your children on the simple but dynamic truths of how to pray and get results. When they really learn to pray effectually, they have mastered one of the greatest secrets of life.

9. Give your children a clear understanding of the work of demons, and how they can administer fearlessly the power of Jesus Christ and overcome all Satan's bondages.

10. Cause your children to understand to the fullest measure that *Jesus is Lord*, and that every area of each child's life should be brought under His control. He is the Master of all that we do and are!

Chapter 5

HE WHO FINDS A WIFE

The bold living role as husband and father is certainly only half a picture without the bold Bible wife and mother beside you. God gave me my wife, the daughter of an old-fashioned preacher of the Gospel, early in my life. I was only nineteen years old when we met at her father's Wednesday night church service. The Bible says, "He who finds a wife finds a good thing, and obtains favor from the Lord" (Proverbs 18:22 *New American Standard*). Twenty-nine years, five children and two grandchildren later, I am still obtaining the favor of the Lord from the support and love of my wife, Joyce.

Joyce has been the perfect bold living helpmeet for me over the years. What is a helpmeet? She is a co-worker in the Lord with her husband. She is there to support him in every way possible, enabling him to move in the calling the Lord has given him. Together Joyce and I discovered the truths of Proverbs 28:1 that the righteous are bold as a lion. Together that became our watchword as we saw who we are in Christ Jesus because of the precious Lion of Judah.

In the earliest days of my ministry, Joyce would travel with me wherever I went to preach and teach the Gospel. Even as the children began to arrive, we would all travel together as much as possible. When the oldest reached school age, Joyce became a teacher as well as a wife and mother. Through this time, her support and encouragement were a priceless blessing to me.

Once our fourth child, Donnie, reached school age, we had to settle down in one place so that the children could attend a regular school. Although Joyce was no longer at my side for every crusade, her prayer support and love were still my greatest asset.

One thing that I have readily learned to recognize over the years is the manner in which the Lord may speak to my wife concerning our ministry. I have come to greatly respect and appreciate Joyce's sensitivity to the Lord and His Word. I remember one time in particular when her sensitivity led to a major step of faith in our lives.

In the 1950's God led us to minister for some time in Canada. We evangelized considerably in the Canadian prairies before going to Tulsa, Oklahoma, to work with T. L. Osborn. Then in 1960, after all five of our children had been born, my wife suffered a miscarriage. While she was in the hospital recovering and seeking the Lord's face, He spoke to her very clearly. She asked me to come to the hospital to tell me a "very important message."

"Honey, God is calling us back to Canada," she told me in tears. "The people in Canada desperately want and need our ministry. We must plan to go back."

I prayed about the matter earnestly. It certainly wasn't an easy step to take. Joyce and I were both from Oklahoma, and we loved our home state and the many friends and loved ones we had living there. Then the Lord spoke to me as He did to Abraham long ago, "Get thee out of thy country, and from thy kindred, and from thy father's house, unto the land that I will show thee..." (Genesis 12:1).

Together Joyce and I took that step of faith and set out for ministry in Canada. In the nearly twenty years since then, the Lord has blessed and prospered us mightily. And I have continued to be thankful that I have a wife who supports me so boldly in the ministry.

Joyce shares her heart

For the rest of this chapter, Joyce would like to share what she believes it means to be a godly, bold living woman, especially in the home.

"I must speak of my family to explain the burden I have on my heart for a strong Christian home life of peace, privacy, personal worth and spiritual gain. I first began to meditate on God's Word concerning the strong Christian home when I was an eighteen-year-old girl and in the throes of an eleven month depression that I thought would take my life.

"The story of those months of depression is one I have shared with many people over the years that Don has been in ministry. I have delightfully shared it as a contrast to what I know a home and family can be once we understand the truths of bold Bible living. It was during that time that I frantically asked myself: Why was I born? At the time I didn't know that it was for the purpose of fellowship with the Father. That is something that I discovered a few years later in my studies with Don. However, there was one thing that I knew I wanted to do with my life on this earth, if I should survive the depths of that depression. I discovered in those months that the desire of my heart was to have a husband and my own little babies to cuddle. I wanted to establish a home that would be free from the tormenting of the devil that I was experiencing at that time.

"Well, God gave me the desire of my heart for a husband. After the Lord miraculously healed me of those months of depression, I asked Him to bring into my life the man that He had spared me for. How marvelously God answered that prayer.

"I sincerely believe that one of the reasons the Lord so graciously spared my life and restored me to health mentally was to provide a calm well-established refuge and life, first of all for my husband, Don, and then for our children. I knew it was essential to insure the right kind of atmosphere to raise to strong manhood and womanhood the children God gave our union.

"Even though our children are grown now, and I am free to help Don in other areas of God's work, for years our home was my primary ministry. I can hardly overemphasize the urgency I feel along these lines. To be a bold living woman is to first and foremost take heed to the ministry of your husband and children that the Lord has given you. In all of the work that my husband has engaged in over the years—the broadcasts, the writings, the personal counseling, the crusades—I could have given them all precedence over my family. But God has not led me that way.

"God gave me a husband, then children, to minister to and care for in this life. I labored to keep our lives in proper perspective in the will of God. I sincerely believe the Lord gave me a sacred duty and privilege in ministering to my family. God has always made me capable to handle anything that has arisen in that area because He has taught me by His Word, His Spirit and through both experience and observation. I can do all things through Christ who has strengthened me."

The godly woman

"Today, the world is painting a confusing picture of womanhood. There is a struggle between rebellion and godly living that is throwing many women into a quandry. You know, the Bible relates a similar time and struggle in the book of Esther. It is an immensely interesting look at how God views and rewards a certain kind of womanhood.

"In the book of Esther, the Lord gives a clear picture of two women, Queen Vashti and Queen Esther. Vashti is a woman who chooses the way of the world—rebellion. Esther chooses godliness, and through her faith in God and her submission, she receives a great reward.

"The story of Queen Vashti's rebellion begins when King Ahasuerus commands that she come before him during a banquet. While it is true that the king has been drinking wine, nevertheless, he was her husband and her king. There is nothing in the Scriptures to suggest that the king was asking Vashti to do anything immoral. But 'Queen Vashti refused to come at the king's command.' The wise men of the court solemnly noted that Vashti's rebellion would 'become known to all the women causing them to look with contempt on their husbands.' Therefore, because of Vashti's rebellion, she was dishonored and stricken from the courts forever.

"What a remarkable contrast to Vashti is Queen Esther. Esther was, first of all, a godly woman whose trust was in the Lord Jehovah. She was also a woman with a meek and quiet spirit (see 1 Peter 3:4), listening to the direction of her uncle, Mordecai, and to those who were placed in charge of her, for 'she did not request anything except what Hegai . . . who was in charge of the women, advised' (Esther 2:15 *New American Standard*). As a result of her godly and humble attitude, Esther 'found favor in the eyes of all who saw her' and was loved by the king more than all the other women.

"But most importantly, Esther was mightily used of God in saving the entire nation of Israel! When the Jews were threatened with annihilation because of the great wickedness of Haman, Mordecai wisely noted that Esther had attained royalty for 'such a time as this.'

"It was with great courage that Esther called a three day fast among her people and then approached the throne of King Ahasuerus. This could have meant death to Esther, but her faith was in the Lord for His protection. In the end, the nation of Israel was saved, and Esther was given great authority and honor in the kingdom.

"It is important to remember that following the Word of God in our actions and our heart attitude will always result in blessing, not just for ourselves, but for those around us. In her bold and yet humble attitude, Esther became one of the greatest women recorded in the Bible and has continued to receive honor throughout the centuries. While Vashti's name, if even remembered, has been connected with her rebellion and her shame.

"Actually, Vashti's threat to turn the other women in the kingdom away from their husbands is one of the things that we see happening today. Women who have their hearts in rebellion have shown contempt for men in general and their own husbands in particular and have released a spirit of rebellion in our nation. Many women even throughout the world have been caught up in this ungodly spirit. These women have come to look on their husbands and their home lives with contempt. Just as the wise men of King Ahaseureus observed, unless this rebellion is dealt with, it becomes a common malady across the land!

"Under the false call of 'liberation' women are being tempted and beguiled to leave their homes, husbands and children to pursue after their own ways. Isaiah, chapter fifty-three, reminds us that 'all we like sheep have gone astray, we have turned every man (and woman) to his very own way.'

"To turn from the Bible picture of womanhood and go the world's way is an iniquity in the sight of God. It is not 'liberation' but a bondage to Satan and his deceptive scheme to destroy the family.

"I realize that most Christian women who know the Lord Jesus Christ have not gone to the extremes of walking out on home and family. But as Christian wives we must be very careful that the spirit of discontentment that rages among the woman's liberation movement would not find even the smallest place in our hearts or our homes. The Bible admonishes us to be content in all things (Philippians 4:11). This spirit of discontentment is not from God.

"It takes a strong Christian woman to stand on the Word of God in her home. It takes a woman determined to be faithful to Jesus and His Word to her. Satan is subtle in his attack, roaming around 'seeking whom he may devour' (1 Peter 5:8). He may attempt to reach you through other women who paint your life as one of drudgery or seek to cause jealousy to rise up within you because of a worldly definition of 'freedom.' But it is the Son and His truth that truly set us free! (John 8:32, 36). Remember what rebellion did for Queen Vashti!

"Christian women, stand boldly on the Word of God. Provide support for your husbands and godly training for your children. Attain to an attitude of meekness and quietness which is precious in the sight of God. This does not mean that you will not be used in bold Bible action. Remember Esther who was mightily used of God. Through bold living, she saved the entire nation of Israel! God's reward to you will be as much a blessing as it was for Esther who found favor in the sight of her peers, her husband and her God!"

LIBERATED!

Ladies, if you have received Jesus Christ as your personal Savior and confessed Him as Lord of your life, you are assured of a life of absolute liberation!

1. "If the Son therefore shall make you free, ye shall be free indeed" (John 8:36).

2. "Ye shall know the truth, and the truth shall make you free" (John 8:32).

3. "When he, the Spirit of truth, is come, he will guide you into all truth" (John 16:13).

4. "The law of the Spirit of life in Christ Jesus hath made me free from the law of sin and death" (Romans 8:2).

5. "Now the Lord is that Spirit: and where the Spirit of the Lord is, there is liberty" (2 Corinthians 3:17).

6. "Thou hast broken the yoke of (our) burden, and the staff of (our) shoulder, the rod of (our) oppressor" (Isaiah 9:4).

7. "But now being made free from sin, and become servants to God, you have your fruit unto holiness, and the end everlasting life" (Romans 6:22).

8. "The Lord shall preserve thee from all evil: he shall preserve thy soul. The Lord shall preserve thy going out and thy coming in from this time forth, and even for evermore" (Psalm 121:7-8).

9. "He hath sent me ... to proclaim liberty to the captives, and the opening of the prison to them that are bound" (Isaiah 61:1).

10. "Stand fast therefore in the liberty wherewith Christ hath made us free, and be not entangled again with the yoke of bondage" (Galatians 5:1).

Summary: The Lord has liberated you, ladies. Do not become entangled once again in bondage to Satan through the deception that is going abroad in the world. Jesus has set you free. His Word declares it!

Chapter 6

CHALLENGING YOUNG PEOPLE

This is the age of the spectator. How many times have you watched the big sports events, the Super Bowl, the World Series, the Olympics and wished you were in there and taking part?

There are also two sides in the arena of the Christian faith: spectator Christianity or bold Bible living. Each of us, adult or teenager, has to make that decision for ourselves. But I would like to speak a word of bold challenge especially to the young people.

In the Christian faith, many young people have developed a spectator Christianity in which few speak out and many barely listen. However, Jesus is calling us to be participants. Jesus *was* and *is* a Man of action, and action He demands. Don't give in to being a spectator. The Christian spectator becomes critical, timid, cold and unproductive. Don't be an observer on the sidelines. Plunge into the stream of life for the Lord Jesus Christ. You will certainly be on the winning side!

Paul Harvey, famous Chicago ABC news commentator, once said, "Youth are looking for a leader, a

flag, a slogan. Youngsters today are desperately
seeking to find out who they are. They are eager to ally
themselves with a cause. They need something to be
for, a reason for being; and they wait for Christianity's
answer.''

I fervently believe that the message of bold Bible
living, the truth that Jesus Christ leads followers to a
rich, full, rewarding life of confidence, courage and
brave action, is a waving banner that youth will
follow.

Someone may ask, ''How do we come by this
boldness you talk about? How can we have this joy,
this faith that we seem to have missed along the way?''

Before Pentecost, the disciples felt just about the
same way. They were discouraged, depressed, defeated, fearful and apologetic. But they received knowledge, the most thrilling and transforming knowledge
that they could know.

This was the knowledge that their Lord had risen
from the dead! That He had conquered death, hell,
and the grave! That He was alive!

With this knowledge they tarried until Jesus filled
them with the irrestible power of the Holy Spirit.

Then, they marched out and acted on that
knowledge and power. They turned the world upside
down for Christ. They wrote the most beautiful
literature in existence—the New Testament. They
made kings and nations tremble. They cast out devils
and brought God's healing power to the sick and
diseased. They were conquerors!

These disciples had dared to expose their lives to
the fire and control of the Holy Spirit, and into their
lives Christ poured spiritual energy they never

dreamed existed. Christ had given them a built-in boldness and a dynamic purpose for living.

This one thing I know: Your faith will never be daring and challenging if you tuck Christ away in a little idealistic compartment of your heart. Christ must be first in everything. Then life will be changed for you, and you will be changed for life. This is the Life that wins.

Rafer Johnson, the amazing young, black runner who set a world record for the 100-meter race in the Moscow Decathlon Competition some years ago, had great insights into the life that wins. Representing the United States, he outran the Soviet Union's fastest runner, Vasily Kuznetzov.

Rafer Johnson testified after the event: "I think three things are essential in athletics. One is being physically ready for competition. Athletes have to be at their peak.

"The second point is the mental attitude. If you think you will lose, you have already lost. Mental training is a tremendous part of an athlete's conditioning. Records are broken because athletes think they can do it.

"But without the Lord's help and guidance through each event, even though I am physically and mentally fit for competition, I would not perform up to my capabilities. That is why I consider it so important to be spiritually ready and sharp.

"In the long run, this third aspect, spiritual conditioning, is really the most important. For here is something we can keep with us and can be a part of us as long as we live; something we can give to others in any phase of life. Ever since I became a Christian in my junior year of high school, I have loved Jesus Christ with all my heart. He is the leader of my life, and without Him I would be lost. Without His help I could not participate in athletics as I do.

"I won't be remembered as a world record holder and Olympic champion, because in a few years there will be more champions. But I will always be able to look back to the days of competition and see the golden thread of the Lord Jesus' leadership.

"Win or lose, I am a member of the greatest team that was ever formed, the winning team coached by the Lord Jesus Christ."

That is a testimony of a fruitful life lived boldly for the Lord.

Don't give in to being a spectator. Be a participant in bold Bible living. Live courageously! Get out in the arena of life for Christ! Be an ambassador in action for Jesus!

Real faith can never exist without acting on God's Word. You can do what God says you can do. Use your faith vigorously. Surrender your life completely to Christ and His Lordship right now!

One major thing that often holds young people back from taking up this bold challenge is the great pressure from their peers. It is difficult to be called different and to be made fun of for not conforming to the ways of the world. Here is where bold Bible living really comes into action in the nitty-gritty of life. It is much easier to go along with the crowd than to stand up for a different way of living.

However, Paul said in Romans 12:2, "Be not conformed to this world: but be ye transformed by the renewing of your mind." As your minds are renewed in Christ Jesus and in biblical principles, it will be easier to stand against the world's conforming forces.

A few years ago, young people that chose not to conform to their peers were called "squares." In more recent times, they have been called other names, including "straights," especially those who refused to be involved with drugs. Whatever the term may be, it all means the same thing: different, peculiar. That should not surprise any Christian, for the Word says, "Ye are a chosen generation, a royal priesthood, a holy nation, a *peculiar* people ..." (1 Peter 2:9). We are a peculiar people because we have chosen to refuse or turn from the world's ways and to be sanctified or "set apart" for the Lord.

The above verse in 1 Peter goes on to say that we are set apart that we might show forth the praises of Him who has called us out of the darkness and bondage of the world into His marvelous light. Stand your ground boldly, and do not let yourself be pulled into bondage again.

I dare you to be a nonconformist. I dare you to disagree with the devil and to agree with the Lord's will and purpose for your life.

One day Jesus walked by the Sea of Galilee and called four young men—Andrew, Peter, James and John—to follow Him. Jesus was interested in young men who would step forth with Him and dare to be nonconformists. Men who would dare to be dynamic in their faith.

When Peter and John, with their brothers, walked off and left a thriving business as fishermen to follow a man who had no place to lay his head, the other fishermen probably thought they had really gone off the deep end. Little did they realize that these brothers would soon become fishers of men. Little did they realize that Peter would preach messages that would cause thousands to accept Jesus as Messiah and Deliverer. Nor did they realize that John would write some of the most beautiful and inspiring literature ever written in his Gospel and the book of Revelation.

The world might call these men "peculiar," but Jesus called them apostles. These same men, without Bible colleges, modern transportation, radios or churches, went forth in daring faith and turned the world upside down and right-side-up; they institutionalized a revolution that led to the downfall of the Roman Empire; they launched the building of a Kingdom that would never be destroyed.

And what of the young man with the Roman citizenship, fine education and high standing in religion—this man called Paul? How do you suppose Paul's friends felt as he began to preach the very faith he had worked so diligently to destroy? Why, he even had the attention of governors and kings. They called him mad, but Jesus called him a "chosen vessel."

What a man this Paul was! He was the one used of God to most clearly interpret what bold Bible living means. Read his epistles such as Romans, Ephesians, Philippians, and his letters to young Timothy. The pages of his epistles leap with confidence and fearlessness; they abound with action and conquest.

It was Paul who endured beatings, imprisonments, shipwrecks, and every known opposition. He was so bold in the Lord that they could not stop him. God was for him, for he was on the Lord's side and in the

Lord's army.

Look at Paul in Acts 27:25 as he stands on the crumbling deck of the disaster-ridden ship and courageously cries out, "Sirs, be of good cheer: for *I believe God!*"

Dare to be like Paul who, when he was no longer a young man, could say to another young man in the faith, "I have fought a good fight, I have finished my course, I have kept the faith: Henceforth there is laid up for me a crown of righteousness, which the Lord, the righteous judge, shall give me at that day: and not to me only, but unto all them also that love his appearing" (2 Timothy 4:7-8).

Now, what about you, young friend? Will you dare to be called names by the people who know nothing of the true values in life? Will you stand strong and be a fisher of men?

Only you can answer these questions. If your answer is yes, you have the assurance of being more than a conqueror by our mighty Lord Jesus Christ who loved you and gave Himself up for you in sacrificial death. He says to you, "Greater is he that is in you, than he that is in the world" (1 John 4:4). God has greater things for you. A greater life to be lived. A life of bold rugged faith!

Christ assures you that He will be with you always, even unto the end. You can boldly say with the apostle Paul, "I can do all things through Christ which strengtheneth me" (Philippians 4:13). I know this is true, because I have seen it proven many times in my own life.

I entered the ministry as a very young man, so I was only 22 years old when the Lord taught me this valuable lesson on walking boldly in Him. I was serving as an assistant to Evangelist William Freeman at the time, and I had been assigned to be the afternoon speaker and platform manager for the massive Freeman Campaign. A man named Bob Wiberg from Indiana was to be the song leader.

Opening night came. Several thousand people filled the Coliseum. The organist was playing appropriate music while the audience filed in. When the starting time was fifteen minutes away, I began to look eagerly for the arrival of Mr. Wiberg, the song leader.

Five minutes later, I left the platform to inquire at the back of the stage if Bob had arrived. Then, with only five minutes before the campaign was to open, I broke out into a sweat. No song leader—what was I to do?

All of my young years, and now as an adult, I have wished that I could sing. While I acknowledge with gratitude the other talents the Lord has given me, singing sweetly is not one of them. And in those early years, with my nervousness, I'm sure my voice was even worse.

Suddenly, I was aware that I had no choice. I would open the campaign, then I must lead the song service. I breathed a quick prayer, then affirmed Philippians 4:13, "I can do *all* things through Christ which strengtheneth me." This has been my battle cry in more than one fierce spiritual struggle. Even as a young and inexperienced person, I was going to live by this Word of Philippians 4:13.

I confessed it over several times, then briskly walked up the steps to begin the service. I made it through the fifteen or twenty minutes of leading that crowd in singing unto the Lord!

It so happened that the song leader never did arrive for that campaign. It fell my lot to lead every song service, afternoon and night, for five solid weeks. Yet, it was a tremendous beginning for me, for in the more than twenty-five years that have followed, I have had to lead hundreds of song services all over the world.

I'm still not the best singer around. However, I refuse to say "I can't" when "I can do all things through Christ!" And I was no different from any young person seeking to serve God. In whatever He calls you to do, you can do it through His strength.

All of these things are part of bold Bible living. Living for Christ in a day when the world is falling apart. Allowing the victorious and mighty Jesus Christ to reign as Lord of your life and to follow Him rather than the world.

This mighty conquering Christ will put courage and purpose in your life. He is the answer for everything. Let Him come into your heart and give you joy, strength, victory, poise, and a happy wholesomeness you never dreamed existed.

You have a whole, wonderful, rich life ahead of you. Give it to the Lord. Let Christ be your Master! Walk boldly in the midst of a crooked and perverse generation as a victor in Jesus.

KEPT FROM SATAN'S POWER

We are living in the days of the devil's wrath. As young people, you may be faced with unusual pressures. But you have been given promise of victory in every trial, and preservation from Satan's power.

1. "In all these things we are more than conquerors through him that loved us" (Romans 8:37).

2. "God is faithful, who will not suffer (allow) you to be tempted above that ye are able; but will with the temptation also make a way to escape, that ye may be able to bear it" (1 Corinthians 10:13).

3. "The Lord knoweth how to deliver the godly out of temptation" (2 Peter 2:9).

4. "For since He Himself was tempted in that which He has suffered, He is able to come to the aid of those who are tempted" (Hebrews 2:18 *New American Standard*).

5. "My grace is sufficient for thee: for my strength is made perfect in weakness" (2 Corinthians 12:9).

6. "I am not asking you to take them out of the world, but to keep them safe from

Satan's power" (John 17:15 *The Living Bible*).

7. "Be of good cheer; I have overcome the world" (John 16:33).

8. "Whatsoever is born of God overcometh the world: and this is the victory that overcometh the world, even our faith" (1 John 5:4).

9. "Resist the devil, and he will flee from you" (James 4:7).

10. "And the God of peace shall bruise Satan under your feet shortly" (Romans 16:20).

11. "Surely he shall deliver thee from the snare of the fowler (trapper), and from the noiseome (deadly) pestilence" (Psalm 91:3).

12. "Be not overcome of evil, but overcome evil with good" (Romans 12:21).

13. "Let us hold fast the profession of our faith without wavering; for he is faithful that promised" (Hebrews 10:23).

14. "Thou shalt be steadfast, and shalt not fear" (Job 11:15).

15. "Who gave himself for our sins, that he might deliver us from this present evil

world" (Galatians 1:4).

16. "Ye are of God, little children, and have
overcome them: because greater is he that is
in you, than he that is in the world" (1 John
4:4).

Summary: In response to these assurances from
God, your heart should overflow with bold
confidence. These are challenging days to serve in
the Kingdom of God. I challenge you to live
boldly as a young man or a young woman for the
Lord!

WHAT I CONFESS, I POSSESS...

Chapter 7

WORDS WORK WONDERS

Several years ago, Pat Robertson invited me to place our daily Bold Bible Living radio program on his vast Christian Broadcast Network, with five stations in New York State and one in Virginia. This was the beginning of a beautiful love relationship with the people of New York, Virginia and Ontario, Canada.

While we often have had fierce challenges of faith for finances to meet our commitment to this Network, it reached a climax in March, 1978. We had to pay $13,400 by the end of the month or else our broadcasts would be discontinued. From March 22 until March 29, approximately $8,000 was received. Then came the last twenty-four hours before the deadline of March 31st; we were about $5,500 short.

Hundreds of people in New York State and elsewhere joined me in a triumphant "watch with thanksgiving." Boldly, we confessed the faithfulness of God to supply our needs. We rejoiced in our confession of the Word, "Thanks be unto God, *which always causeth us to triumph in Christ*" (2 Corinthians 2:14). How we all held our hearts and our confession steady, believing for the balance of the $13,400.

It was one of the sweetest moments of our lives when Joyce and I sent off by Special Delivery mail exactly $13,400 on that evening of March 31, 1978. That God will always cause us to triumph in Christ Jesus was the confession that brought us on to victory!

How important to bold Bible living are our words? I have been in ministry for more than 26 years now. And I believe the greatest secret that God has taught me on bold Bible living, that has produced such momentous wonders, has been the power of our spoken words.

I have put my fingers in the ears of people who were totally deaf, many of them didn't even have an eardrum. Putting my fingers in those ears, I have spoken the words, "In the name of Jesus, I command spirits of deafness to leave these ears. In Jesus' mighty name, I command the hearing to come in strong and normal." The results have been miraculous. Most of the people have been completely healed so that they can even hear the smallest ticking of a tiny wristwatch!

It overwhelms me when I consider the wonder of it! Just by the words of authority, in the name of Jesus, creative miracles can take place. Physical substance is created in a moment's time as words are spoken.

This shouldn't be as strange to us as it seems, for it was by His very words that God created the world. It is by words that we are recreated in Christ Jesus. So we are ourselves word products; the products of God's own wonderful, omnipotent words. Now, when we speak His words, it is simply acting upon the authority God has given us.

We have been instructed in God's Word to "hold fast the profession (confession) of our faith without wavering; for he is faithful that promised" (Hebrews 10:23). As we hold fast to the confession of the Word, we are to "affirm constantly" those things that God has revealed to us (Titus 3:8).

But what is confession? Is it merely when we admit to wrong doings in our lives? The word "confession" in its positive meaning in the Bible means "to say or affirm what God has said in His Word about a certain thing." It is agreeing with God. It is saying the same thing the Scriptures say. To hold fast our confession is to say what God has said over and over again until the thing desired in our heart and promised in the Word is fully manifested. There is no such thing as possession without confession.

When we discover our rights in Christ given throughout the Bible, we are to affirm them constantly. Testify to them. Witness to these tremendous Bible facts. The apostle Paul said that the communication of our faith would become effectual (would work) by our acknowledging every good thing which is in us in Christ Jesus (Philemon 6). Therefore, our faith will only be effective as we confess with our mouths all the good things which are ours because we belong to Jesus.

The Psalmist said, "Let the redeemed of the Lord say so..." (Psalm 107:2), and again, "Let such as love thy salvation say continually, Let God be magnified" (Psalm 70:4).

We know that in Jesus Christ we have been given salvation, not just for our souls, but for our bodies in our health, our finances, our peace of mind and our freedom from bondage and fear.

Affirmations of these truths should ring from our lips constantly. We are told to hold fast to them without wavering. The penalty for wavering in our confession is that we deny ourselves God's promises and the performance of them. "But let him ask in faith, nothing wavering: for he that wavereth is like a wave of the sea driven with the wind and tossed. For let not that man think that he shall receive any thing of the Lord" (James 1:6-7).

Boldly say what God says

Make God's Word the standard for your life. Train yourself to say what He says. Bring your lips under subjection. Think before you speak. *Say what God says!* Don't contradict Him and His Word. God is in His Word. When you confess it, He performs it! Sooner than you can imagine, a revolution will take place in your life. You will find that you are truly living the bold, abundant life set forth in God's Word. I know this for certain because it has happened innumerable times in my own life and ministry.

I have been blessed over and over as I remember how God undertook for us in our mission to Africa several years ago. We were down to the last day before leaving and we were still $1700 short of the necessary funds for our air tickets. No matter what avenue I had pursued in obtaining the money, all of them remained steadfastly closed. But I knew that this was the time to hold my heart steady in expectation that God Himself would minister to our need. I quietly reaffirmed over and over in my heart and with my mouth what the

Word has promised, "My God shall supply all my need according to his riches in glory by Christ Jesus" (Philippians 4:19).

Arriving at our office, Joyce and I agreed together that we would trust the Lord—just as we have boldly preached to thousands of others to do. So we gathered our staff together and joined hearts and hands as we presented the need of $1700 to our heavenly Father. Then we lifted our hands and praised the Lord in advance for His supply. We began to confess the Word together and went on doing our normal duties of the day.

While I was gone from the office, a man from Vancouver called to tell us that the Lord had laid it upon his heart to provide $1700 for our air tickets! This was one of the most miraculous interventions we had ever experienced. The Lord used that man to minister the exact amount of money we needed! We had employed the only resources we had: our faith in God, which we expressed by our words of confession for His supply. We had spoken words of faith, had utilized words of prayer, had employed words of praise and confession of the Word, and now we were seeing God's response by a tremendous miracle!

Indeed words spoken in harmony with God's Word work wonders. The Lord says, "To him that ordereth his conversation aright will I show the salvation of God" (Psalm 50:23). We are not mere robots without a choice of the words we speak. While we want God to guide our conversation, to motivate our words, we still have the choice to order our conversation aright or to order our conversation wrong. So God says, "If you choose to order your conversation aright, I will show you My salvation." That salvation is in every area of our lives.

Several years ago, we took a group of Christians to Israel where I served as the head tour guide. As soon as we left Jerusalem to journey through Samaria and Galilee, I was suddenly stricken with a severe fever. Naturally, experiencing a high fever like that is quite a drain on your body system; it actually makes you feel less than human. It was quite a battle for me.

I knew that I shouldn't talk about it to the friends I was leading through Israel. I would certainly get their sympathy and pity and might begin to feel sorry for myself. That would not help me at all. What I needed was a healing from God. I must maintain my confession of His Word in the face of my dire need.

As I disciplined my heart and lips and continued to confess, "with his stripes I am healed" (Isaiah 53:5), the Lord manifested a beautiful healing for me at Nazareth. Jesus of Nazareth became my personal Healer of a fever that had raged in my body. How grateful I was for His love! I would like to say to you that need healing for your body: Discipline your lips to hold fast your confession of God's Word, saying often, "with His stripes I am healed."

It is essential that we take the Lord's strength for any weakness we may have and confess that strength daily. In ourselves we are aware of our weaknesses. Paul was aware of his own weakness. Yet, he also knew that when he was weak, then he became strong in the Lord's own strength (2 Corinthians 12:10).

We all know our weaknesses in life. Sometimes our weakness is in our conversation, some bad habit, an overindulgence in television or eating, or some other thing that does not glorify God. Whatever our weaknesses are, the Lord knows how to minister strength. Let's confess His Word, "The Lord is the strength of my life" (Psalm 27:1). Say the words of Joel 3:10, "Let the weak say, I am strong." Say it over and over again, "In Jesus I am strong! I am strong!" If that seems like a contradiction to your own natural thinking, consider that you're moving to a higher level where God's Word prevails, not your own negative feelings and thoughts.

The Christian life is often made up of a series of adversities and problems, which God always gives us the grace to overcome. That is why God calls us to be overcomers, not those who go under. When we hold our heart steady in praise and confessing the Word, no matter what the circumstances, God will see us through.

So I challenge you, "Don't talk sickness, rather speak the healing Word. Don't talk weakness, rather affirm that the Lord's strength is yours. Don't talk defeat, rather shout your victory in Jesus. Don't talk lack, rather confess His provision for your every need. Don't talk bondage, rather confess His freedom.

With the mouth you make confession unto healing, deliverance and every spiritual and physical blessing provided for you in Jesus Christ. By your words, you even overcome Satan. Revelation 12:11, "And they overcame him (Satan) by the blood of the Lamb, and by the WORD OF THEIR TESTIMONY."

Words can work blunders!

Words work wonders, but they can also work

91

blunders!

Did you realize that multitudes of people fail in life because they talk failure... they fear failure... they really believe in failure?

What you say locates you. You will not—you cannot—rise above your own words. If you talk defeat, fear, failure, anxiety, sickness, unbelief, you will live on that level. Neither you, nor anyone else, no matter how clever, will ever live above the standard of your conversation. This spiritual principle is unalterable.

If your conversation is foolish, trifling, impractical or disorganized, your life is invariably the same way. With your words, you constantly paint a *public* picture of your *inner self*. Jesus said, "Out of the abundance of the heart the mouth speaketh" (Matthew 12:34).

When you think back on your life, you will probably agree that most of your troubles have been tongue troubles. The Bible says, "Whoso keepeth his mouth and his tongue, keepeth his soul from troubles" (Proverbs 21:23). Oh, the trouble caused by unruly tongues. Words spoken in the heat of the moment, words of anger, words of harshness, words of retaliation, words of bitterness, words of unkindness... these words produce trouble for us.

Beloved, let's make it our prayer right now, "Let the words of my mouth, and the meditation of my heart, be acceptable in Thy sight, O Lord, my strength, and my redeemer" (Psalm 19:14). Here's another good Bible prayer, "Set a watch, O Lord, before my mouth; keep the door of my lips" (Psalm 141:3). It is really important that we let God help us overcome our unruly speech habits, for our words can work blunders and get us into much trouble.

A negative confession precedes possession of wrong things. The Bible warns, "Thou art snared with the words of thy mouth, thou art taken with the words of thy mouth" (Proverbs 6:2). With the mouth confession can be made, not only to the good things God has promised us, but with the mouth confession can be made unto sickness, defeat, bondage, weakness, lack and failure.

Refuse to have a bad confession. Refuse to have a negative confession. Repudiate a dual confession where you are saying at one moment, "By His stripes I am healed," and at the next moment, "But the pain is still there." Your negative confession denies the healing scripture, and you go on in defeat.

Higher level living

Go on to higher level living in the Kingdom of God. Believe you are what God says you are. Think that way. Talk that way. Act that way. Train yourself to live on the level of what is written in God's Word about you.

Do not permit your thoughts, your words or your actions to contradict what God says about you.

Although you may not master the secret of the positive confession of God's Word in a day, or even a week, you *will* learn it as you continue to walk in it faithfully.

Jesus commanded us to "have faith in God"—or to "have the God kind of faith." Then we are told that "faith comes by hearing...the Word of God." After you hear the Word, then it begins to possess your *heart* and *mouth* as Paul says, "The word...is even in thy *mouth*, and in thy *heart*" (Romans 10:8).

When a sinner is converted, first, he *believes* on the Lord Jesus Christ and that God raised Him from the dead; then his *confession* is made unto salvation (Romans 10:10).

God fulfills all His promises the same way.

First: You hear the promise—that creates faith. *Second:* You believe that promise. *Third:* You confess that promise; you talk it; your overflowing heart confesses the Word of promise in gladness and assurance. *Fourth:* You act accordingly, and God delights to make it good.

So, meditate on the Word of God and all that it has to say for every aspect of your life. As the Word becomes a part of your heart, it will set you free from fear and anxiety and build you up in bold Bible living. Then the abundance of your heart will supply the words of your mouth automatically. Your confession is really a natural overflow of what springs from your innermost being...your heart.

Now, with the truth of God's Word held deep in your heart and springing from your lips, you can freely discover for yourself the wonder of your own bold words!

Chapter 8

WE MAY BOLDLY SAY

As we launch out in bold Bible living, learning to confess God's Word in the midst of all our situations, we need to see exactly why we have the right to make those confessions. We know that we have a right to boldly confess God's Word because of Hebrews 13:5-6: "For He hath said, I will never leave thee, nor forsake thee. So that we may boldly say, The Lord is my helper."

Notice: "*For He hath said . . .* so that *we may boldly say.*" It is because of what "*He* hath said" that "*we* may boldly say."

Because He hath said, "I am the Lord that healeth thee" (Exodus 15:26), we may boldly say, "Yes, Lord, I am in health because You are the Lord that healeth me."

Because He hath said, "Whoso offereth praise glorifieth me" (Psalm 50:23), we may boldly say, "I am glorifying my Creator by praising Him."

Because He hath said, "Man shall not live by bread alone, but by every word that proceedeth out of the mouth of God" (Matthew 4:4), we may boldly say, "I have esteemed Thy Word more than my necessary food."

Let no thoughts dwell in your mind that contradict what "He hath said." You just "boldly say" the same thing.

God says of His own Word, "For I am the Lord: I will speak, and the word that I shall speak shall come to pass.... The word which I have spoken shall be done, saith the Lord God" (Ezekiel 12:25, 28). You can count on God's Word being good. It cannot fail without God failing.

The Lord has also said, "So shall my word be that goeth forth out of my mouth: it shall not return unto me void, but it shall accomplish that which I please, and it shall prosper in the thing whereto I sent it" (Isaiah 55:11).

The following sections are all part of God's Word that He has sent forth to accomplish His purposes. Because "*He* hath said" these things, "*we* may boldly say" them, knowing the Lord will accomplish the purpose of His Word. Hallelujah!

Because He hath spoken, we know we can declare it boldly; it will be as He has said because, "There hath not failed one word of all his good promise, which he promised" (1 Kings 8:56).

We may boldly say:
GOD IS FOR US
Because He hath said, "I am come that they might have life, and that they might have it more abundantly" (John 10:10), we may boldly say, "I have that abundant life in me now because I have received Jesus Christ as Lord."

Because He hath said, "If God be for us, who can be against us?" (Romans 8:31), we may boldly say, "God is for me and no one can succeed against me."

Because He hath said, "Whosoever therefore shall confess me before men, him will I confess also before my Father which is in heaven" (Matthew 10:32), we may boldly say, "Jesus is confessing me right now to the Father because I am confessing Him before men."

Because He hath said, "When the enemy shall come in like a flood, the Spirit of the Lord shall lift up a standard against him" (Isaiah 59:19), we may boldly say, "God's Spirit is raising a mighty standard of defense in my behalf at the very time the enemy is heaping his pressure on me; praise the Lord, my case is His."

Because He hath said, "Thy God whom thou servest continually, he will deliver thee" (Daniel 6:16), we may boldly say, "God is my deliverer in every case because I constantly serve Him."

Because He hath said, "The Lord is nigh unto them that call upon him...in truth" (Psalm 145:18), we may boldly say, "The Lord is near me now because I call upon Him in truth."

Because He hath said, "The Lord shall fight for you, and ye shall hold your peace" (Exodus 14:14), we may boldly say, "I know God is fighting for me because I am holding my peace; I have committed the battle into His hands."

Because He hath said, "Thanks be unto God, which always causeth us to triumph in Christ" (2 Corinthians 2:14), we may boldly say, "I am more than a conqueror through Christ who loves me."

Because He hath said, "No good thing will he withhold from them that walk uprightly" (Psalm 84:11), we may boldly say, "The Lord is withholding no good thing from me because I am walking upright before Him."

Because He hath said, "There is therefore now no condemnation to them which are in Christ Jesus" (Romans 8:1), we may boldly say, "I have no condemnation because I am in Christ."

Because He hath said, "Casting all your care upon him; for he careth for you" (1 Peter 5:7), we may boldly say, "I am carefree because all my cares are cast upon the Lord."

Because He hath said, "Him that cometh to me I will in no wise cast out" (John 6:37), we may boldly say, "I have come with my sins, burdens and failures, and the Lord has taken me in."

Because He hath said, "Commit thy way unto the Lord; trust also in him; and he shall bring it to pass" (Psalm 37:5), we may boldly say, "The Lord is working out every detail of my life because I have made a committal of it all to Him, and I am fully trusting Him."

We may boldly say:
HEALING IS OURS
Because He hath said, "Beloved, I wish above all things that thou mayest prosper and be in health, even as thy soul prospereth" (3 John 2), we may boldly say, "I have a right to prosperity and health because I am prospering in my soul."

Because He hath said, "Himself took our infirmities, and bare our sicknesses" (Matthew 8:17), we may boldly say, "I am free from sicknesses and disease because they were all carried by Jesus Christ for me."

Because He hath said, "He that raised up Christ from the dead shall also quicken your mortal bodies by his Spirit that dwelleth in you" (Romans 8:11), we may boldly say, "God is quickening my mortal body now by the very same Spirit that raised Jesus from the dead because His Spirit dwells in me; thus, I am free from weakness and sickness."

Because He hath said, "They shall lay hands on the sick, and they shall recover" (Mark 16:18), we may boldly say, when we lay hands on the sick, "They are recovering because I am acting on His Word."

Because He hath said, "Ye shall serve the Lord your God, and he shall bless thy bread, and thy water; and I will take sickness away from the midst of thee" (Exodus 23:25), we may boldly say, "Sickness is taken away from me, my bread and water is blessed because I am serving the Lord my God."

Because He hath said, "Unto you that fear my name shall the Sun of righteousness arise with healing in his wings" (Malachi 4:2), we may boldly say, "The Lord is arising with healing for me now because I fear His name."

Because He hath said, "He sent his word, and healed them" (Psalm 107:20), we may boldly say, "Healing is mine now; the Lord is healing me through His Word because I have received His Word into my life."

We may boldly say:
OUR PRAYERS ARE ANSWERED
Because He hath said, "Before they call, I will answer; and while they are yet speaking, I will hear" (Isaiah 65:24), we may boldly say, "The Lord is answering my prayer even now as I pray. In fact, He was already working on the answer before I prayed."

Because He hath said, "Go thy way; and as thou hast believed, so be it done unto thee" (Matthew 8:13), we may boldly say, "I can be on my way; I have prayed and believed; the answer will come just as I am expecting."

Because He hath said, "Call unto me, and I will answer thee, and show thee great and mighty things, which thou knowest not" (Jeremiah 33:3), we may boldly say, "The Lord is answering me and showing me great things because I am calling unto Him."

Because He hath said, "Whatsoever ye shall ask in my name, that will I do, that the Father may be glorified in the Son'' (John 14:13), we may boldly say, "The Father is being glorified in the Son because He is doing great things for me as I ask in His name."

Because He hath said, "Delight thyself also in the Lord; and he shall give thee the desires of thine heart" (Psalm 37:4), we may boldly say, "The Lord is granting me the desires of my heart because I am delighting myself in Him."

Because He hath said, "If ye abide in me, and my words abide in you, ye shall ask what ye will, and it shall be done unto you" (John 15:7), we may boldly say, "I am abiding in Christ, He is living in me, and He is answering my petitions."

Because He hath said, "Ask, and ye shall receive, that your joy may be full" (John 16:24), we may boldly say, "My joy is full because I am asking and receiving in Jesus name."

Because He hath said, "What things soever ye desire, when ye pray, believe that ye receive them, and ye shall have them" (Mark 11:24), we may boldly say, "I shall have what I have prayed for because I have prayed for it and I believe it is mine even now."

Because He hath said, "Every one that asketh receiveth" (Matthew 7:8), we may boldly say, "I know I am receiving because I have asked; 'everyone' means no exceptions—it includes me."

UNTROUBLED HEARTS

If your heart is filled with fear, you will talk fear, and your fears will increase. The amazing thing is that when you speak, those fears immediately grip you tighter than ever.

To overcome this, fill your heart with the Word of God. Then, when you are tempted to doubt, make your lips speak His Word instead of your doubts. Simply make a decision to have your lips voice the Word instead of fear. You can do it through the Lord Jesus Christ who will give you the strength (Philippians 4:13).

Because He hath said, "Fear thou not; for I am with thee: be not dismayed; for I am thy God" (Isaiah 41:10), we may boldly say, "I am no longer afraid because God is with me all of the time."

Because He hath said, "God hath not given us the spirit of fear; but of power, and of love, and of a sound mind" (2 Timothy 1:7), we may boldly say, "I am free from all fear because my God hath not given me fear, but power, love, and a sound mind."

Because He hath said, "My peace I give unto you. . . . Let not your heart be troubled" (John 14:27), we may boldly say, " 'Being justified by faith, we have peace with God through our Lord Jesus Christ' (Romans 5:1), for He is our peace (Ephesians 2:14), and therefore my heart is not troubled or fearful."

Because He hath said, "Thou wilt keep him in perfect peace, whose mind is stayed on thee: because he trusteth in thee" (Isaiah 26:3), we may boldly say, "I have His perfect peace because my mind is stayed on Him."

OVERCOMING EVIL

I shall not have a wrong confession or a bad confession. A wrong confession is giving place to Satan. I have stopped talking defeat, sickness and weakness. Defeat is of the devil. Weakness is of the devil. As long as I am speaking about these things, I am praising Satan's works and not God's!

Because He hath said, "Resist the devil, and he will flee from you" (James 4:7), we may boldly say, "The devil if fleeing from me because I am steadfastly resisting him in Jesus' name."

Because He hath said, "Ye shall know the truth, and the truth shall make you free" (John 8:32), we may boldly say, "I am set free because I know His blessed truth."

Because He hath said, "In my name shall they cast out devils" (Mark 16:17), we may boldly say, "Devils are going out because I have commanded them to go in Jesus' name."

Because He hath said, "The Lord shall deliver me from every evil work" (2 Timothy 4:18), we may boldly say, "I will not fall into any of the devil's evil snares; the Lord delivers me."

Because He hath said, "The angel of the Lord

encampeth round about them that fear him, and delivereth them" (Psalm 34:7), we may boldly say, "The angel of the Lord makes camp around me to deliver me and to protect me because I do fear the Lord."

Now that you have all of those Scripture verses before you, practice agreeing with God. Accept what He says for your own victorious, bold Christian walk. Believe you are what He says you are. Believe you can do what He says you can do. Believe God is what He says He is and that He will do and *is doing* what He says in His Word.

Think of yourself like God thinks of you. Remember that because *"He* hath said...*we* may boldly say!" Now walk in your bold living victory!

Chapter 9

TO THE THRONE BOLDLY

When I first moved into the Gospel ministry full-time, I was a guest at the home of some friends. One day I was playing with their five-year-old son, who persistently begged me to swing him around by holding to his arms.

Picking him up suddenly, I felt his little bones break right in my strong hands.

His parents were terrified. They rushed him to the doctor's office in a nearby small town. The doctor took X-rays and came out with a disheartening verdict: "The boy's left arm is so badly broken that major surgery will be required to set the bones. I am not equipped to perform that operation here. I'll call the nearest hospital and request they prepare for surgery."

We rushed the boy to this hospital, fifty miles away. He was seated between his parents in the front seat; I was alone in the back seat. I felt sick at heart to think that I had actually broken his arm in the accident and that now this little fellow faced surgery.

Aware of the gravity of the situation, I took my New Testament from my pocket to read. John 16:24 fell open in front of me, "Ask (in my name), and ye shall receive, that your joy may be full!"

With tears in my eyes, I prayed, "Lord, what full joy it would bring to us if You would heal this broken arm, even as we journey now. In the name of Jesus, I ask You to heal this broken arm and make it every whit whole."

When we arrived at the hospital, the doctors were ready for surgery. First, however, they needed to take their own X-rays to determine how to operate. In about fifteen minutes, they returned with baffled expressions on their faces. They showed us the X-rays; no indication at all of any broken bones!

While these fine physicians were astonished, we had "fullness of joy" that Jesus had miraculously intervened and healed the boy's broken arm!

Hallelujah! What jubilation we had! How we thanked the Father for hearing and answering our prayer!

"I love the Lord, because he hath heard my voice and my supplications. Because he hath inclined his ear unto me, therefore will I call upon him as long as I live" (Psalm 116:1-2).

I love the Lord! There are many reasons why I love the Lord. I love the Lord because He first loved me (1 John 4:19). I love the Lord because He has saved me, healed me, called me to preach His Gospel.

But with David, the Psalmist, I wish to be specific in another area. "I love the Lord, because he hath heard my voice and my supplications." This is a supernatural wonder: our voices are heard in heaven. When we pray, we are not merely talking off into space . . . we are communicating with the great God of this universe. Heaven bends low to hear our voices.

Jesus, at the tomb of Lazarus, looked up to heaven and said, "Father, I thank thee that thou hast heard me. And I knew that thou hearest me always . . ." (John 11:41-42).

As joint-heirs with Jesus Christ, we can pray with the same sort of boldness and confidence. For you remember that Jesus has said to us, "Whatsoever ye shall ask the Father in my name, he will give it to you" (John 16:23).

We can look up and say, "Father, I thank You that You have heard me, and I know that You always hear me when I pray in the name of Jesus Christ!" Hallelujah! Wonder of wonders! God hears our voices when we pray!

I wasn't always so effectual in prayer or so bold to come before the Father in petition. I would permit Satan to fill my mind with feelings of condemnation or unworthiness. Until something happened with my young son that has been a tremendous help in my own prayer life. I have shared this in the book *Praise Avenue*, but I feel it is important enough to repeat. It deals with the scripture from Matthew 7:9-11, and how it became real to me:

"What man is there of you, whom if his son ask bread, will he give him a stone? Or if he ask a fish, will he give him a serpent? If ye then, being evil, know how to give good gifts unto your children, how much more shall your Father which is in heaven give good things to them that ask him?"

One morning at an early hour, I was on my knees in the kitchen of our home "trying to pray through." But

107

there was no victory, joy, nor blessing for me in that prayer time. For too often this has been my dismal experience.

Then my little son, Michael, only about eighteen months old at the time and just beginning to walk and talk, found me there in the kitchen. He quietly snuggled up beside me, put his baby arms around my neck and said, "Daddy, I'm thirsty. I want a drink of water."

Quickly, I arose and got some water and quenched his thirst. Then, I embraced him tenderly and had a captivating time of fellowship with him.

Because it was so early, little Michael wanted to go back to bed. I carried him to his room and was almost overwhelmed by the rapturous knowledge that I was a father and this was my own little boy.

I returned back to the kitchen to resume my prayer time. It seemed so unattractive and dull compared with the precious relationship with my son I had just been enjoying.

Then, so lovingly, so assuringly, the blessed Holy Spirit spoke these words to my heart, ". . . If ye then, being evil, know how to give good gifts unto your children, how much more shall your Father which is in heaven, give good things to them that ask him?"

I pondered over these words. They warmed my heart. I was challenged!

I, Don Gossett, a father of the natural order, certainly knew how to give good gifts to my children (we had both Mike and Judy then). I had delighted to give them little presents.

When I was out in evangelistic crusades away from my wife and children, I would usually plan to take some little gift home to them. I would give it thought and care. If I delighted to give good gifts to my own children, *how much more* shall my Father in heaven give good things to them (that included me) who ask Him!

Suddenly, the light had shone from heaven! The Holy Spirit had illuminated my mind and heart. Never again would I pray with the feeling that my Father didn't care or that I was unworthy.

No! I was His child, dear to Him. He had redeemed me through the blood of His Son Jesus Christ.

Every provision had been made for me to have a joyful, bold prayer life. There stood the door open to the Throne Room: "Let us therefore come *boldly* unto the throne of grace, that we may obtain mercy, and find grace to help in time of need" (Hebrews 4:16).

Hallelujah! Jesus had made the Way where I could come *boldly* to fellowship with the Father in the Throne Room. I could look up to Him lovingly and say "My Father," and I could almost hear Him say to my innermost being "My child."

Never again would I be dull in His presence. I knew He loved me far more than I could ever love even my own children.

Praise God, that was liberation morning for my prayer life!

I am glad that we are serving a prayer-hearing and prayer-answering God and Father.

Psalm 34 is a real commentary to what God does in answer to prayer: "I sought the Lord, and he heard me, and delivered me from all my fears. . . . This poor man cried, and the Lord heard him, and saved him out of all his troubles. . . . The young lions do lack, and suffer hunger: but they that seek the Lord shall not want any good thing. . . . The eyes of the Lord are upon the righteous, and his ears are open unto their cry. . . . The righteous cry, and the Lord heareth, and delivereth them out of all their troubles." All of these great things are brought to pass as we *boldly* pray.

In answer to prayer, I have seen the Lord save and heal multitudes, give jobs, change lives, transform homes, and bless humanity in miraculous ways.

In Japan they have a god called Shintu. This huge, enormous god of stone is constructed with many ears. The poor, deluded people stand and cry out to this dead god of many ears. They bow and scrape, they offer sacrifices, they do everything conceivable to get a response from this god . . . but to no avail.

But we who trust in the living God know that He inclines His ear to us, to hear our prayers.

"And this is the *confidence* that we have in him, that, if we ask any thing according to his will, he heareth us: And if we know that he hear us, whatsoever we ask, we know that we have the petitions that we desired of him" (1 John 5:14-15).

How our hearts should be moved to boldly call upon Him! God declares, "Ye have not, because ye ask not" (James 4:2). "Ask, and it shall be given you; seek, and ye shall find; knock, and it shall be opened unto you" (Matthew 7:7).

I love the Lord because He has done so many glorious things in response to my prayers. And because of that, I am going to continue to call upon Him as long as I live!

"In everything by prayer" is God's admonition.

"Men ought always to pray, and not to faint" (Luke 18:1).

Yes, I do love the Lord because He hears and answers my prayers!

I am going to give you a little exercise that I learned many years ago on growing in our bold prayer life. It is a practical way to begin praying boldly for your needs and seeing answers to your prayers.

Although you could use anything you are praying for that is in accordance with God's will (see 1 John 5:14-15), I am going to use a specific area of concern in this example.

Multitudes of Christians are burdened with this question: How can I see my own loved ones brought to Jesus Christ?

I once had this burden heavy on my heart. But I learned to embrace the promise of the Bible, "Believe on the Lord Jesus Christ, and thou shalt be saved, and thy house" (Acts 16:31). I thank God that through a series of miracles, I saw my entire family, brothers, sisters, parents come to the Lord.

At that time, the Holy Spirit revealed to me the simplicity of receiving answers to my prayers that I would like to pass on to you. He did it through the promises of Jesus in John, chapter 14:13-14, 15:16, and 16:23. In those verses, Jesus gave us the right to use His name.

When this truth of asking the Father in Jesus' name was brought home to me, I saw that Jesus had given us, in effect, a signed check on the Bank of Heaven. And He was saying, "Whatsoever ye shall ask the Father in my name, he will give it to you" (John 16:23).

So I had a check printed up, as you see on the example, and the exciting results have been repeated many times over the years as Christians have learned to pray boldly, believing on the Word of God.

But first of all we need to ask: What is believing?

Real Bible believing is acting on God's Word! There is no such thing as believing without action. James declares that, "faith without corresponding actions is dead" (James 2:26 *Weymouth*).

Faith and believing have only to do with God's Word. As we honor God by acting on His Word, He will honor us by granting our requests and needs.

And remember, it is impossible to ask "too much" from your Father for you have been "blessed with all spiritual blessings in heavenly places in Christ" (Ephesians 1:3).

You come to the Father through Christ. Be definite: don't insult the Father by vague ramblings. Approach the Father as a son, not as a servant or slave.

Your chief desire is that He may receive glory, so you talk plainly before Him. Open your heart, lay your desire before His eyes and make your case clear. Let Him see that it is for His glory.

How to fill in the check

Date the check. On the front side, write in the date you present your prayer request to the Father. This is a key step. You are pinpointing a specific time when you present your needs to the Father in Jesus' name. From that day forward, you hold your heart steady in faith and praise until the answers are fully manifested.

Write your own name on the top line. You are the

THE BANK OF HEAVEN

THE FATHER WILL

Date _____

Give To _____

Whatsoever Ye Ask (Personal) _____

(Others) _____

In the Name of *Jesus*

recipient of the Father's miracles, so be sure to write your name on the top line. Others may be the beneficiaries of your prayers, but you are the one entering into the contract with God's Word.

Write in your request. After the word "Personal" write out your own needs from God. Be specific. Do you need physical healing, a change in finances, a healing for your marriage, a husband or wife? Present your personal requests to the Lord.

Next, write in the needs of others. Here you can include all of your loved ones who are in need of salvation. And you can add the needs of others that you may have on your heart.

Boldly ask the Father. Ask Him specifically for the very things you have listed on the check. Don't pray, "Father, if it be Thy will, save these souls." It is always the Father's will to save souls. God is "not willing that any should perish, but that all should come to repentance" (2 Peter 3:9). Expect the Holy Spirit to start dealing with these souls right now, wherever they are. Believe that they will have receptive hearts to the Spirit's working. And remember that you are always asking in the name of Jesus. It is He who signed the check.

Sincerely thank Him. You have asked the Father in the name of Jesus. Christ said, "The Father will do it." It is being done now. Your part is to begin to thank Him for the answer. Remember, the language of faith is praise and thanksgiving. It is also the language of victory, for *faith is the victory* (1 John 5:4).

Keep the check. Keep this check in your Bible or wallet. Daily hold it up to the Father and thank Him for meeting the needs. Realize that when you fill in the check on the Bank of Heaven you are not playing games. You are engaged in a fight of faith, but faith is the victory.

One woman in Pendleton, Oregon, had written on one of these prayer checks the names of her ten children for their salvation. She kept the check in her Bible and daily she would take it out, hold it up to the Father and praise Him for the answer.

One by one her children began receiving Christ as Savior. She kept on praising God for their salvation. When I saw her two years later, she showed me that same prayer check. She had crossed off eight of the names because eight of her ten children had received salvation. For twenty-seven years she had cried and begged God for the salvation of her children without exercising the faith to believe or thanking God for the answer. Now she was praising through to glorious victory!

The first time I ever preached on the prayer check was many years ago, in the beginning of my ministry. I can remember driving to a Sunday rally and wondering how the people would receive this teaching. But the enthusiasm of the congregation went beyond my expectations, and the first person to present me with a prayer check written on the Bank of Heaven received an astounding answer to her prayer.

A woman came into the prayer line with her check in hand. She desperately needed a miracle healing for two cancers on her head; one on the side of her face and the other on her throat. When I took this woman's check in my hand and started to present her need to the Lord in the name of Jesus, the glory of God came upon her, and she began mightily praising Him. I knew something glorious was happening for this rejoicing woman.

About two weeks later, the same woman came to a meeting I was conducting in another church. She met me in the vestibule before the service with an enormous smile on her face. However, I didn't recognize her. She began to brush her hand across the side of her face and her throat as she continued to walk toward me. Seeing my bewilderment, she hurried over.

"You don't recognize me, do you?" she asked.

"No, I don't," I admitted.

"No wonder," she explained joyfully. "I am the woman you prayed for with the ugly skin cancers. After the rally that day, I returned home. As I was washing my face in the afternoon, I accidentally brushed against the cancer on the side of my face. It fell right out into the palm of my hand, roots and all. A few days later, the skin cancer on my throat dried up and fell off. Now my skin is like a baby's. The Lord has healed me of both cancers!"

This is the result of coming boldly to the throne of grace in your time of need. Learn how to live boldly in your Christian life of prayer!

HOW TO PRAY BOLDLY
AND GET RESULTS

FIRST: Prayer is the way God has appointed that He will work in behalf of humanity. God will do little or nothing unless we ask Him (James 4:2). He says, "Call unto me, and I will answer thee" (Jeremiah 33:3). Bold prayer is simply asking God and *expecting* to receive the answer!

SECOND: "Come *boldly* unto the throne of grace, that we may obtain mercy, and find grace to help in time of need" (Hebrews 4:16). This is the Bible way to come to God: *With boldness*, which means confidence and assurance that you are welcome. Then remove from your life hindrances to receiving answers—an unclean heart and a wrong spirit. Confess your sins to God (1 John 1:9), and ask Him to renew you with a right spirit (Psalm 51:10).

THIRD: Who can pray and get results? Paul did. So did Daniel, David, Elijah and Abraham. Why? "The effectual fervent prayer of a righteous man availeth much" (James 5:16). But who is righteous today? You are! Knowing that you are righteous is the greatest foundation for a prayer life that gets results. Your being righteous is based only on what Jesus has done for you (2 Corinthians 5:21; Romans 10:10). As a righteous person, you have influence with God!

FOURTH: "The effectual fervent prayer of a righteous man availeth much." Gets results! What does it mean to be righteous? It means you have the ability to stand in God's presence without any sense of sin, guilt or unworthiness. Into God's presence you come boldly through the blood of Jesus (Hebrews 10:19).

FIFTH: Pray about everything (Philippians 4:6). Dare to ask God for miracles (John 16:23-24). "When ye pray, believe that ye receive them, and ye shall have them" (Mark 11:24). Only believing prayer gets results from God. Ask the Father in Jesus' name. Then believe you shall receive . . . and you shall have! Now shift from praying to praising! You are fully persuaded that what God has promised, He will perform! (Romans 4:21).

SIXTH: Cease struggling: you have committed your need into God's hands. Rest in the sure promise of God. You have "planted" your request by prayer; "water" it with much praise; expect God to give the "increase!" (1 Corinthians 3:6). And He will!

GOD GIVETH ME WEALTH
AND HEALTH ...

Chapter 10

LIBERALITY IN GIVING

The most joyful Christians are those who know the blessing of *bold giving*. They dare to respond to God's Word, to see the Lord do what He says He will do . . . "I am the Lord, I change not . . . PROVE ME now herewith (with your tithes and offerings), saith the Lord of hosts . . . I WILL open you the windows of heaven, and pour you out a blessing, that there shall not be room enough to receive it. And I will rebuke the devourer for your sakes" (Malachi 3:6, 10-11).

I dare you to put God to the test in your giving. When you give in this manner, God has given you permission to affirm boldly, "I am proving my God. He is pouring me out an overflowing blessing. He is rebuking the devourer for my sake!"

Harry Wiltbanks was one of the most successful Christians I have ever known. His testimony for Christ was strong and influential. During one crusade, Joyce and I stayed in his home. One day he told us his "success" story.

Coming out of World War I without God and penniless, he received Christ as Lord and Savior.

Reading the Bible, he began to take God's Word at face value. He asked the Lord for a job and got one. He read God's promises concerning giving and began to tithe and give offerings, too. He was undenying in his faith...God *must* bless him, spiritually and financially. God is not a man that He should lie! Harry Wiltbanks began to receive abounding blessings! This continued through many years...the man giving scripturally, and God pouring forth His blessings. The result was that by giving, Harry was instrumental in winning multitudes of souls all the time. Now he is home with the Lord, reaping his reward.

The Bible says that when we give, we are honoring the Lord. The result again is God's promise that He will reward you with *plenty* (Proverbs 3:9-10). When you give of your substance, recognize that you are actually "honoring the Lord," and you can expect the reward of "plenty" as God blesses you materially.

What is *bold giving*? It is liberal giving (Proverbs 11:25); bountiful giving (2 Corinthians 9:6); cheerful, ungrudging giving (2 Corinthians 9:7); blessed giving (Acts 20:35); devil-defeating giving (Malachi 3:11).

What is the blessing of bold giving? It not only opens the windows of heaven (Malachi 3:10), but its reward is "given unto you; good measure, pressed down, and shaken together, and running over, shall men give into your bosom" (Luke 6:38). God promises you plenty shall be your reward, spiritually and materially. But most importantly, your bold giving sends the Gospel forth to the winning of souls and the meeting of needs.

The opposite of bold giving is *fearful giving*. "I was afraid to trust God's Word for many years," a

Christian man told me. "Fear compelled me to give dimes when I should have given dollars. I found no joy in giving because of this spirit. Finally, I began to give cheerfully, liberally, ungrudgingly. How abundantly God began to bless me! I indeed found the blessing of *bold giving*, and how my Christian life was transformed!"

Dare to abandon yourself to God's promises in your giving. You will not only "lay up treasures in heaven," but you will experience tremendous joy here below. I have known many blessed people in my life that have had the courage to give liberally in this manner and have seen God do wonderous deeds in response to their obedience to His Word. One such man was my friend, Evangelist Velma Gardner of California. His testimony of tithing has always blessed my heart.

"We were in the heart of the depression. My father died and left no insurance, so it fell on my older brother and my lot to provide for our mother and five brothers and sisters. Men by the thousands were out of work. We were so poor that every morning, as I started to look for work, I would have to put cardboard inside my shoes to keep my feet off the ground. I couldn't afford five cents for shoe strings, so I used wire to keep my shoes on.

"One day a friend came and said, 'I think I can get you a job in a big box-factory.' I was really thrilled. Hundreds of men daily were trying to get a job there, but he got me in. We were twenty-five miles from home at this factory and stayed in a little cabin by the river. I started to work for the tremendous sum of twenty dollars a week, which was really a lot of money in those days. God spoke to me all week about tithing.

"When I came home that Saturday night I said, 'Mother, I feel that I should tithe. I know we're poor and need all I can earn, but I want to go on with God.'

"My mother cried, and said, 'Son, you walk with God; He will take care of us.'

"On Sunday morning I gave two dollars for my tithe and that night I put one dollar offering in the basket. Oh, how happy I was that I had obeyed God. Immediately, he began to bless my soul; the air seemed fresher, the grass greener, the flowers prettier, the birds sang more sweetly. I felt better. Why? Because He was opening the windows of heaven upon my soul.

"I went happily to work the next day, and, when I arrived at the plant, there stood the foreman, waiting to see me. They called him 'Old Grump'. No one had ever seen him smile. He was the terror of the whole crew. He hollered, 'Come here, you.'

"The devil sneaked up and said, 'Now don't you wish you had that three dollars to get back to town on? You're fired!'

"With fear and trembling, I stood before 'Old Grump'. With a very stern look on his face he said, 'I've been watching you work.' Then I was really scared.

"He continued, 'We just bought a new electric box-making machine, the first ever invented. My boy will operate it and you will be his assistant. You'll receive an increase in pay of 33⅓ percent.'

"I shouted, 'Hallelujah!' so loud in my soul that the devil nearly fell over himself getting away from me!

"Saturday night, when I returned home, I joyfully

announced, 'Mother, God has proven Himself; I got a raise!'

"That Sunday I had more tithes to pay and a bigger offering to give. The next Monday morning I went back to work and, to my horror, there the boss stood again.

"The devil said, 'Now listen, you can just shove me so far, then I start in. You had to testify about what God did when you started tithing, so now you have lost your job. This is the end.'

"With fear and trembling, I stood before the boss. He almost smiled as he said, 'We just bought another machine yesterday; you can operate this one. You will get twice as much money as you have been receiving.' The devil left on roller skates for hell!

"Within six weeks I was making more money than any man that had been there for twenty years, including the boss himself. Don't tell me it doesn't pay to tithe.

"God will bless you financially, spiritually and physically. Since that time, God has blessed me with health. He has taken care of my every need, and the windows of heaven are still open and His blessing is thrilling my soul. I would not stop tithing for anything in the world.

"Luke 6:38 says, 'Give, and it shall be given unto you; good measure, pressed down, and shaken together, and running over!' He will give you what you deserve, then He will press it down, shake it together and run it over. No wonder David said, 'My cup runneth over.' Yours will, too, if you give to God.

"I can still remember when I was just a small freckled-faced boy, headed for the little country grocery store. I would walk up to the candy counter longingly and say, 'Gimme a penny's worth of jelly beans!' The old groceryman's heart would move with compassion, and he would take a small bag and fill it up with nice red and black jelly beans. As I saw the bag fill up, I had only one ambition in life, and that was to get behind that counter, take that bag and gently shake it. I knew if I could, I'd be able to get a few more black jelly beans in! I wanted all I could get.

"Friends, that is exactly what God will do. He will press it down, shake it together and run it over. Hallelujah!"

Many Christians today run into the problem of believing that tithing is right in their hearts; yet they listen to the devil's protests that with the rise of the economy—food prices, housing, clothing—they could not possibly afford to tithe and still provide for their families. Believe me, that is a lie from the father of lies himself. Especially in this day and age of the "failing dollar," we cannot possibly afford *not* to tithe. In a time when Satan's inflation is running rampant in the world, we only have God on our side to rebuke the devourer as we tithe in obedience to His Word. There is no stronger foundation, no greater surety in this time of financial difficulties than the Word of God. But sometimes it takes quite a bit for the impact of God's Word to reach some individuals.

There is the testimony of one dear country preacher who learned the faithfulness of God's Word in an unusual way. He explained to his congregation how God dealt with him concerning the importance of tithing.

"Many years ago when I was a country missionary, the famous Baptist businessman, H. Z. Duke, who founded the Duke and Ayers Nickel Stores over a wide area, came to this county. Speaking to Christian laymen, he urged men and women everywhere to try God and see if He would not make good His promises to bless them in material things when they gave tithes and offerings to His cause. After Mr. Duke had spoken at one community, I took him in my buggy to another community. Mr. Duke said to me, 'Brother Kuykendall, do *you* believe in tithing?'

" 'I certainly do,' I said. 'I believe in tithing and I preach it myself.'

" 'But, Brother Kuykendall,' he continued, 'do you *practice* tithing?'

"Sadly, I had to answer, 'No, I do not. I believe in tithing, but I cannot practice it. You see, I have thirteen children at home. Every meal fifteen of us sit down at the table. I receive only $125 a month, $1500 a year salary. (Even many years ago that was a meager amount.) I have to maintain my own horse and buggy for constant traveling. It is just impossible to take care of all the needs of a family of fifteen out of $125 a month and have money left to tithe. So I believe in tithing, and I preach it, but I cannot practice it.'

"Mr. Duke was a very kindly man. He said, 'Brother Kuykendall, would you like to tithe? Would you tithe if I back you up financially so you could be sure you would not lose by it?'

" 'Nothing would please me more,' I said.

"So Mr. Duke made me the following proposition:

" 'For the next year, I want you to set out to give God at least $12.50 every month, as soon as you get your salary. Then, if you feel led, you may give more. I promise you that if you need help, I will give it. Simply write me a letter and say, 'Brother Duke, I'm giving a tithe, but I miss the money. I need it for my family. I've given so much thus far.' I promise you that I will send you a check by return mail. Are you willing to try tithing on that basis?'

"I hesitated a moment, moved with emotion, and Brother Duke said, 'I have thirty-two stores. I have plenty of money to make good my promise. I will be glad to do it. Will you risk me and start tithing on my simple promise that I will make good any amount you've given, any time that you find you miss it and need it? Will you trust me about it?'

"I gladly accepted his offer. I said, 'Yes, Brother Duke, I've wanted to tithe for a long time, but I felt I simply could not do it. Now, thank God, I can tithe, and I'll be glad to. And I will not feel like a hypocrite when I tell others they ought to tithe.'

"So I started tithing for the first time in my life. Every month I took out, first of all, one tenth of my salary and gave it to the Lord's cause; then, as I felt led, I gave more. In the back of my mind, I always had this thought, 'Mr. Duke promised me he would simply make it up any time I need it. He will send me the money if I simply ask him for it.'

"But a strange thing happened. It seemed our money went farther than before. I would preach in some county community and somebody would tie a crate of chickens on the back of my buggy. Somebody would put a ham under the seat. Or a godly woman would put some home canned fruit in my buggy.

"A neighbor farmer said, 'Brother Kuykendall,

God has blessed me so much that I cannot get all my corn in the crib this year. I have an extra wagon load that I cannot keep. May I put it in your crib for your buggy horse?'

"Another neighbor drove over with a great hay wagon full of hay for the cow.

"It was very strange, but that year we had no doctor bills. The children's clothes didn't seem to wear out so quickly. It was a happy time. I never yet had to call on Mr. H. Z. Duke to make up the money I had given to the Lord in tithes.

"Then one day when the year was almost gone, and the test was about over, I suddenly realized with shame that I had believed what H. Z. Duke had said. He promised to make good anything I lacked by tithing, and I believed him. But my heavenly Father had made the same promise, and I had not believed *Him*! I had taken the word of a man when I did not take the promise of God! Now I had proven God's promises and found that He took care of me and my big family on a small salary. I found that $112.50 per month took care of our family better, with God's blessing, than $125 did without being under the blessed covenant which He has made with those who seek first the Kingdom of God through tithes."

That godly country preacher stood there before the congregation weeping. With deepest emotion he said,

"Now I have tithed for many, many years. My salary has increased year after year. We've always had enough. We've never been shamed. The greatest spiritual blessing of my life, aside from salvation, has been in learning to trust God about daily needs for my home and our big family."

God has proven to everybody who has ever tried Him that He would keep His promise. He provides for those who bring Him the first fruits, those who give tithes and offerings, those who boldly seek first the Kingdom of God and His righteousness, allowing the Lord to add blessings of abundance to their lives!

LIBERALITY IN GIVING

As you meditate on these dynamic words of God, you are assured that through liberality in giving, you can experience the joy of bold Bible living.

1. "Inasmuch as ye have done it unto one of the least of these my brethren, ye have done it unto me" (Matthew 25:40).

2. "Whosoever shall give you a cup of water to drink in my name, because ye belong to Christ, verily I say unto you, he shall not lose his reward" (Mark 9:41).

3. "He that giveth unto the poor shall not lack" (Proverbs 28:27).

4. "If thou draw out thy soul to the hungry, and satisfy the afflicted soul; then shall thy light rise in obscurity, and thy darkness be as the noonday" (Isaiah 58:10).

5. "Bring ye all the tithes into the storehouse, that there may be meat in mine house, and prove me now herewith, saith the Lord of hosts, if I will not open you the windows of heaven, and pour you out a blessing, that there shall not be room enough to receive it" (Malachi 3:10).

6. "The generous man will be prosperous,

and he who waters will himself be watered"
(Proverbs 11:25 *New American Standard*).

7. "Every man according as he purposeth in his heart, so let him give; not grudgingly, or of necessity: for God loveth a cheerful giver" (2 Corinthians 9:7).

8. "Be ye strong therefore, and let not your hand be weak: for your work shall be rewarded" (2 Chronicles 15:7).

9. "Blessed is he that considereth the poor: the Lord will deliver him in time of trouble" (Psalm 41:1).

10. "God is able to make all grace abound toward you; that ye, always having all sufficiency in all things, may abound to every good work" (2 Corinthians 9:8).

11. "He that hath pity upon the poor lendeth unto the Lord; and that which he hath given him will he pay him again" (Proverbs 19:17).

12. "Give, and it shall be given unto you; good measure, pressed down, and shaken together, and running over, shall men give into your bosom. For with the same measure that ye mete withal it shall be measured to you again" (Luke 6:38).

SUMMARY: You now know that God promises you prosperity and plenty because you are liberal in giving unto Him. This makes your giving a noble privilege! Have you praised Him for enabling you to be a bold Bible giver?

Chapter 11

QUEST FOR THE BEST

Do you know that there are many sincere tithers who don't realize that they are ready for God's next financial step in their quest for the best?

Because we live in a materialistic world where money is the primary medium of exchange, having enough money to make ends meet is the constant challenge of most people's lives.

Joyce and I became parents of five children young in life. In fact, we were both only twenty-eight years old when our youngest, Marisa, was born.

Being responsible for so many mouths to feed presented unusual demands for money. More money than I usually had. My wife became very ill, and in the months before the Lord healed her, I had to take a break from the ministry and stay home to take care of my wife and children. Not knowing how else to handle the problem, I went into debt.

Years later, even after the Lord had taught us the principles of tithing discussed in the previous chapter, and we were finally seeing our way to His material blessings, we often remained in debt for one thing or another, especially as it involved the ministry. But then, in the mid '60's, the Lord began to speak to our hearts about being in debt. He used several different people to reveal to us His will on finances. I was preaching one time in the city of Chicago when the Chicago Tribune carried an article that caught my eye. It was a testimony from a woman who had been happily married for fifty years.

"I know why John and I have been happy these fifty years," she said. "In the first place, we have made it a rule never to go into debt. I have lived in Chicago sixty-eight years and never during that time have I owed one person a cent...

"I believe a good deal of unhappiness is caused by spending more than you make. It has been our policy to buy what we could well afford to have, and then stop."

What this woman, who wasn't necessarily even a Christian, had to say really spoke to me. I quickly remembered what the Bible said to confirm and support what had brought her so much happiness over the years. In the Word there is a general rule laid down respecting the meeting of obligation. "Render therefore to all their dues: tribute to whom tribute is due; custom to whom custom.... *Owe no man any thing*, but to love one another" (Romans 13:7-8).

When one goes into debt he is not rendering what is due to the person that he owes. Even beyond that, he places himself under a certain bondage. "The borrower becomes the lender's slave" (Proverbs 22:7 *New American Standard*).

At the same time that I read the article by this lovely lady from Chicago, I came in contact with some of the wisest words I had ever heard spoken on the subject of debt by T. DeWitt Talmage, the famous preacher:

"Debt! There is no worse demoralizer of character. Debt ruins as many households and destroys as many fine characters as rum. Pay all your bills. Look every man in the face, conscious that you owe the world no more than it owes you.

"This running into debt is a great cause of dishonesty. Young men (and women) are growing quite shameless about being in debt, and the immorality extends throughout society. Tastes are becoming more extravagant and luxurious, without the corresponding increase of means to enable them to be gratified. But they are gratified, nevertheless, and debts are incurred, which afterwards weigh like a millstone around the neck.

"The safest plan is to run up no bills, and never to get into debt. And the next best is, if one does go into debt, to get out of it again as quickly as possible. A man in debt is not his own master; he is at the mercy of the tradesmen he employs.

"No man can be free who is in debt. The inevitable effect of debt is not only to injure personal independence but, in the long run, to inflict degradation. The debtor is exposed to constant humiliations."

I believe that the testimony of the woman from Chicago and the advice of Brother Talmage are both excellent in applying to our personal lives.

Painfully, Joyce and I took the challenge in light of the Word, "I can do all things through Christ which strengtheneth me." Our source was Christ. Our testimony was founded in His Word, "I can do all things . . ." We applied it to our personal situation of being in debt. "I can do all things through Christ who enables me. I can pay my old debts through Christ's ability."

With that determination, and with the assurance that God would never expect anything of us that He wouldn't enable us to do, we got out of personal financial debt. We did it, but it didn't happen over night. For instance, I owed an auto repair firm $150. Each week for seventy-five weeks I mailed two dollars to them. That was the best I could do, and I did it through Christ who enabled me.

You ask, "If Christ did it through you, why didn't He provide the whole $150 at once?"

I don't have the answer for that. I asked Him for the money, and He provided it in His own way. I believe, in that case, He was allowing me to develop persistence and patience in my faith. Other debts He provided for miraculously, like the time he saved my car, at the last possible moment, from repossession. But whichever way the Lord chose to do it, I never wavered or doubted that I would pay that car repair debt and many similar debts.

Within less than two years, I was personally debt-free!

There is no reason why every single person reading this book cannot experience the same glorious freedom from debt. It is a great God that enables us to do all things through Christ Jesus! He upholds His Word that we would owe no man anything but love by providing all of the means necessary, no matter what they are, to free us from the bondage of debt. Whom the Son sets free shall be free indeed! (John 8:36).

At this point, I would like to add that I am not

necessarily referring to such things as houses or cars in this chapter. I believe that the purchase of those items—which is generally done on a time-payment plan—is solely up to the individual Christian as he is personally led by the Spirit of God. "For as many as are led by the Spirit of God, they are the sons of God" (Romans 8:14).

In being debt-free, the story for the Gossetts didn't end with our own personal finances. We were privileged, through the ministry, to see the Lord do much greater things. As God began to set us free from our personal debts, we realized that the same principles apply for the Lord's work! In the Bible we have several good examples on financing the Lord's work (Exodus 35:4-9, 1 Chronicles 29:2-9, 2 Kings 12:4-12). In each instance, it is important to notice that the means were provided before the work of building was begun. The people offered willingly to the Lord in each of these Bible accounts, and there was great joy.

So the Lord began to speak to our hearts about having a debt-free ministry for the Gospel of Jesus Christ. We knew that it wouldn't be easy. Actually, it was often a fight of faith. But we agreed strongly with Dr. Talmage . . . Debt is a demoralizer. It affects your freedom. We wanted to be as free as possible to preach and reach out with the Word of God. It is not the Father's will that ministries which glorify the name of His Son should be exposed to the humiliations caused by debt.

We presented the matter fervently to the Lord in prayer. Then we took some active steps to clear up all the outstanding debts. We even set a time limit on the matter, believing the Lord that we would soon be able to operate our World Ministry under the guidance of God, free of the dangers inflicted by debt.

How the Lord was faithful! He supplied our needs for the ministry through so many different people and in so many different ways that it never failed to make me stop in awe and thanksgiving for the all-powerful and loving Father that we have!

Giving still the key

Now, in believing God for the means to get out and remain out of debt, the central key to His provision is still our liberality of giving. Are you in debt because the devourer has gotten hold of your finances? Remember that when we rob God, the devourer has a free place in our lives. But when we honor God with the first fruits of our substance, He rebukes the devourer for our sakes and provides the money (or whatever else necessary) to have our needs met and much more! Then there is no reason to be in debt is there?

In preaching on this subject of the importance of owing no man anything, I have often been asked the question: "If God wants me to pay my debts, then isn't it wrong to be giving part of my money away? Shouldn't I pay off my debts first, and then pay my tithes with a free conscience?"

In case you have the same question, I would like to let Wade C. Smith, a famous newspaper columnist, answer that question with his own personal story.

"If a man owed me money, and he was having a

hard struggle to make a living, and by all common sense there appeared to be very little prospect of ever getting my money back, I would try to persuade that man to begin tithing.

"I confidently believe if I could induce him to tithe his income, that is, pay one-tenth of it to the Lord, he would sooner or later pay back every cent he ever owed me because he would prosper.

"Tithing solved serious financial problems for me and, at the same time, brought me spiritual blessings that far outweighed the material gain.

"When I began tithing twenty-one years ago, I was hopelessly in debt. Misfortune, which came when I first began to be a wage earner, plunged me deep 'in the red.' In trying to work it out, repeated misfortunes came one after another. So that, like a frog endeavoring to escape from the well, when I jumped up two feet, I fell back three.

"That was awfully discouraging, and I had just about given up hope of ever getting out of debt—when I was persuaded to begin giving to the Lord one-tenth of what I earned.

"When I was first challenged to tithe, I almost smiled; it seemed so ridiculous for me to think of it. Why, I said, it would be dishonest for me to 'give away' any part of my income to church, or anything else, when I owed money to those who had trusted me. Before I could give away my money, I must pay my creditors.

"But I was troubled, for I was a Christian, and I knew that tithing was scriptural, that the Bible stated a definite portion (one-tenth) should be paid to the Lord.

"So I prayed for light and understanding as to what really was duty in my own 'particular' circumstances. Then this startling fact came to me: The Lord is my first creditor! 'Will a man rob God? Yet ye have robbed me. . . . In tithes and offerings' (Malachi 3:8).

"If any creditors should be given preference, it was the Lord. He certainly had the first claim on me.

"Then I looked further in Malachi 3:10, and I saw God promising that if I would trust Him and tithe, He would open the windows of heaven and pour out a blessing so big there would not be room enough to receive it. So I decided to begin tithing, and I nailed the purpose down with Malachi 3:10.

"On the first of the following month when I drew my salary, I took one-tenth and put it aside for the Lord's work. During the first two months, it was pretty hard, and I had to pray harder and hang on harder to Malachi 3:10.

"It looked for a little while as if God had forgotten about opening the windows. But I set my jaw and hung on. I kept a careful account to be sure that I was fair to God, even to the penny.

Then things began to come to pass!

"Ways came to me to earn more money—ways I had never dreamed before. Altogether unexpectedly, my salary was increased. I don't have the space here to detail the different means for making more money that suddenly came to me.

"In less than a year, I was out of debt and buying my own home. Up to that time, I had lived in a rented house. I even saved up something against old age.

"That was all wonderful, but the greatest joy of all

was the dispensing of the 'Lord's tenth.' It grew to much more than a tenth—more than double that amount.

"Formerly, it made me grit my teeth to hear a missionary sermon or any appeal for money for the church or for charity—I was so hopelessly in debt!

"But now I rejoiced for every clear call from the Lord for His work, because there was always something in the Lord's treasury, and I was His trusted servant to hand it out.

"How I wish somebody would have told me this story when I was fifteen. How much joy I have missed!

"How much financial misery I have suffered! How different it could have been if I had just known! Before I began to tithe, financing seemed to have a curse attached; since I began to tithe, it is full of blessing.

"For twenty-one years I have not worried about money. Oh, sometimes there is close figuring, but it is always with the consciousness that the Lord, my Senior Partner, and I are figuring together, and I know it will work out—and it does."

Perhaps today is one of the most difficult times in history to seriously consider living a debt-free life. There is an ever-increasing trend towards obtaining everything that we desire—*now*! Credit is so easy to come by that many major retailers are offering as much as $1000 in instant credit, with a supplemental plan not to start payments on the debt until two or three months later! While Satan and his world-system are luring the public with such appealing temptations, we, as Christians, must take a bold stand in opposition to what the world is offering.

The NBC television network recently did a special on the peril of credit cards. There was a time in my own life when I was so poor that I almost had a craving for a credit card, just to be able to have one. That was a real status symbol of success and "having arrived." Then the Lord blessed and prospered us in the ministry, and, in a short time, I was able to get all the credit cards I wanted. Now, I find that as I travel credit cards are a means to keep from carrying a lot of cash and to help me in my bookkeeping procedures. But the imminent danger of buying what we cannot afford or succumbing to a spur of the moment temptation by Satan must always be guarded against. The documentary on NBC was a real shocker, even with my awareness of what the enemy is trying to do to bring indebtedness to this nation. I have personally made it a policy to use my credit card only as a means of convenience when traveling. We never allow the bill to go beyond the thirty-day payment, so that we pay on the principle, without having to pay any interest. It is only a means of serving my business interest.

Our credit cards should never control us. If they ever begin to, we should destroy them immediately. Satan's way would be to keep God's children in bondage to debt. But in bold Christian living, we can stand courageously against the enemy's ploys and be free in every area of our lives!

If you have had problems with indebtedness, but you wish to pursue God's quest for the best by being debt-free, I suggest that you take these steps:

1) Pay your tithes and offerings. Do not rob the very God whom you are asking for help (Malachi 3:8).

2) Pray, asking God to provide for your needs adequately so that you can meet your present obligations as well as take care of your past indebtedness. Then stand on His Word, "My God shall supply all (my) needs according to his riches in glory by Christ Jesus" (Philippians 4:19).

3) Make an effort to pay even a small amount on your past debts; see a Christian financial counselor if you need the extra help. Sooner than you can imagine, you will pay off those debts even by small installments. "I can do all things through Christ which strengtheneth me" (Philippians 4:13).

4) Continue to rejoice that the Word of God is true and can be depended upon. God has promised that His Word will not return void, but will accomplish His purposes! (Isaiah 55:11).

ARE YOU WORRIED
ABOUT FINANCES?

Worry about money problems! How often I experienced this worry in the past. Has worry over financial matters robbed you of your song of joy? God's Word assures us of freedom from financial worries. Read these sixteen reasons why you need never worry again about finances.

1. "My God shall supply all your need according to his riches in glory by Christ Jesus" (Philippians 4:19).

2. "Ask, and it shall be given you; seek, and ye shall find; knock, and it shall be opened unto you" (Luke 11:9).

3. "Consider the ravens: for they neither sow nor reap; which neither have storehouse nor barn; and God feedeth them; how much more are ye better than the fowls!" (Luke 12:24).

4. "Casting all your care upon him; for he careth for you" (1 Peter 5:7).

5. "The Lord will give grace and glory: no good thing will he withhold from them that walk uprightly" (Psalm 84:11).

6. "Your heavenly Father knoweth that ye

have need of all these things" (Matthew 6:32).

7. "Hitherto have ye asked nothing in my name: ask, and ye shall receive, that your joy may be full" (John 16:24).

8. "Fear not, little flock; for it is your Father's good pleasure to give you the kingdom" (Luke 12:32).

9. "Trust in the Lord, and do good; so shalt thou dwell in the land, and verily thou shalt be fed" (Psalm 37:3).

10. "I have been young, and now am old; yet have I not seen the righteous forsaken, nor his seed begging bread" (Psalm 37:25).

11. "If ye then, being evil, know how to give good gifts unto your children, how much more shall your Father which is in heaven give good things to them that ask him?" (Matthew 7:11).

12. "But rather seek ye the kingdom of God; and all these things shall be added unto you" (Luke 12:31).

13. "A little that a righteous man hath is better than the riches of many wicked" (Psalm 37:16).

14. "Even the very hairs of your head are all numbered. Fear not therefore: ye are of more value than many sparrows" (Luke 12:7).

15. "If then God so clothe the grass, which is today in the field, and tomorrow is cast into the oven; how much more will he clothe you?" (Luke 12:28).

16. "Your Father knoweth that ye have need of these things" (Luke 12:30).

Summary: As we live by John 3:16 for assurance of salvation, we can boldly live by these blessed verses to have provision for every financial need. Expect daily fulfillment of these words of God as long as you live! This is the God of Provision who can get you out of debt and keep you there! Praise Him!

Chapter 12

RULER OVER MANY

Athletics have always interested me greatly. As a youth I was an active competitor in basketball, baseball, football, boxing and track. The discipline required and the persistence necessary for winning are similar to the bold Christian life.

In 1950 the Associated Press took a poll to determine who was the greatest athlete of the 20th century, or the past 50 years to that time.

When all the poll results were in, the runaway winner was Jim Thorpe, who excelled in track, football, hockey, lacrosse, basketball and baseball. He outdistanced such men as Babe Ruth, Jack Dempsey and Red Grange.

I never knew Jim Thorpe personally, but I always admired his feats in athletic competition, especially his unmatched records in the Olympic games. Jim was a Cherokee Indian from Oklahoma. Since I too was born in Oklahoma with a healthy part of Cherokee Indian blood, I have had an extra interest in this great man.

When Jim astounded the world by his superiority

at the Stockholm Olympics, Gustavus V, the King of Sweden, told Jim Thorpe, "You, sir, are the greatest athlete in the world!" To which Jim replied, "Thanks, King."

When you and I, as Christians, do our best and are faithful to the job the Lord has given us to do, we will hear King Jesus say one day, "Well done, thou good and faithful servant, enter thou into the joy of thy Lord!"

That will be the day of days!

The Lord Jesus spoke of a similar day in His parable of the talents in Matthew, chapter twenty-five.

There was a wealthy man who was traveling to a far country and leaving some of his riches behind with his servants. To the first servant he gave five talents (a form of money in that day), to the second servant he gave two talents, and to the third servant he gave only one talent. The Bible is clear to point out that the lord gave the gifts "to every man according to his ability."

While the lord was away, the servants were left as "stewards" over their master's money. The one with the five talents traded them and received five more. The one with the two talents did likewise, doubling his master's riches. However, the third servant was a poor steward and merely buried his portion in the ground. What happened when the master returned from his long journey? To the man with the five talents and to the other with the two talents, the lord said, "Well done, thou good and faithful servant: thou hast been *faithful over a few things,* I will make thee *ruler over many things:* enter thou into the joy of thy lord" (Matthew 25:21). But to the servant with the one talent who had simply buried the money in fear of his master, the lord said, "Thou wicked and slothful servant. . . . Thou oughtest to have put my money to the exchangers (bankers), and then at my coming I should have received mine own with (interest). Take therefore the talent from him, and give it unto him that hath ten talents. For unto every one that hath shall be given, and he shall have abundance: but from him that hath not shall be taken away even what he hath" (Matthew 25:26-29).

The Kingdom of God is like this today. Our Lord and Master, Jesus Christ, has gone on a journey from which He will return at His Second Coming. In the meantime, the Lord has given each of us our individual talents, abilities, possessions, gifts, callings and purposes in life. To me I know He has given the ministry of World Radio Evangelism; writing and publishing Gospel literature; evangelizing among the Indians and others. To you He has given other gifts, perhaps to sing His glories, to pastor a local church, to witness at your job, to raise a family, to pray for the work of the Lord and so very much more.

Are you being faithful? Am I being faithful? The Lord gave the greatest commendation to the ones who used their "talents" and increased them. But the one who buried his talent or gift in the ground for fear of the master was considered a "wicked and slothful (lazy)" servant.

I certainly don't want to hear that accusation from the Lord on His return. It is my heartfelt desire to hear His words of pleasure to me as His faithful servant. I want to be as the "faithful and wise steward, whom his lord shall make ruler over his household" (Luke 12:42).

It is very necessary to bold Bible living that we recognize the spiritual principle of stewardship. When we are faithful stewards of the things the Lord has given us, no matter how small, our reward shall be authority or rule over large and important things. As we learn how to be faithful in the practical "earthly" aspects of our Christian lives, God will place us as stewards over His spiritual riches as well! Jesus Himself said, "He that is faithful in that which is least is faithful also in much: and he that is unjust in the least is unjust also in much. If therefore ye have not been faithful in the unrighteous mammon (money, possessions), who will commit to your trust the true riches?" (Luke 16:10-11).

The true riches of God's Kingdom, the riches of His Gospel, will only be given to the man or woman who prove themselves faithful stewards of the little things Jesus has given them in the beginning. Paul reinforced this scripture from Luke 16:10 when he exhorted Timothy to commit the truths of the Gospel "to faithful men" (2 Timothy 2:2).

We are to be faithful stewards in every aspect of our lives, materially *and* spiritually. First, let's take a look at our stewardship of material possessions.

Did you know that the material possessions you have actually belong to God? Rather than owning them ourselves, the Lord has made us "stewards" over them. We can bring glory to His name by the way that we take care of His goods. And we will reap the blessings of greater material wealth while we are on this earth if we are faithful stewards.

Joyce and I have seen the workings of this spiritual truth in our own lives. When we began the ministry we had little to call our own. We had no real home, no furniture, and a car that was old and falling apart. But we knew the principle of proper stewardship. As we held our hearts steady before the Lord, we took good care of whatever He had given us. Even that old car was kept clean and shiny as though the Lord Jesus had given it to us Himself. Whatever apartment, hotel room, or place to stay that was temporarily ours, we took great pains to keep it neat and homey—a testimony to the Lord. God gave us grace in this time not to feel sorry for ourselves but to endure hardship as good soldiers and press on.

In due time, lo and behold, we began to increase. The Lord rewarded us with our own little home to care for. What a great victory that was for us! Even though at first we only had a few beds and some old orange crates for a table, the Lord continued to bless us. After several months, He provided the money for a living room suite and soon our house was filled. Through the years since then, we have continued to exercise stewardship over the things God has given us. My wife has taken beautiful care of our home and belongings, and I have done my best to help her and to take good care of our car. Through it all, the Lord has continually shown the tremendous blessings of good stewardship.

One of the most important ways that we can show our faithfulness to God is by being good stewards of our calling or ministry. Remember Paul's admonition to "Take heed to the ministry which thou hast received in the Lord, that thou fulfill it" (Colossians 4:17).

Every child of the King has a ministry unto the Lord. You may say, "Who me? But all I do is work in an office!" or, "All I do is stay at home with my kids!" Nevertheless, every born-again, bold living Christian has a ministry unto the Lord Jesus Christ.

As I mentioned earlier, in the beginning years of my ministry as an evangelist, Joyce and I usually had no place we could call our own. The financial response for our ministry was so meager that often we couldn't afford even to rent a single room to call home.

There were precious people who graciously opened up their homes to us. For a time, we stayed with Ed and Georgia Tharpe. Later, we stayed with Bill Bennett and his wife. The Word makes it clear the special reward to those loving people "who see a need and fill it" by providing room and food for the Lord's servants.

There were other times we didn't have access to homes like the Tharpes and the Bennetts. Tears tend to fill my eyes when I think of the extraordinary kindness of any elderly couple whom we called "Poppy and Mommy" Myers. That's what their own children called them; so did we. They had told us that if we ever needed a place to stay, to come to their home.

One wintry night very late, we arrived in their city from a preaching engagement. Because it was so late, we were hesitant to go to their home. However, we didn't have enough money to rent a motel room. After cruising the streets for a time, we knocked softly at their door. This was to be repeated a number of times during those early years. Always "Poppy and Mommy" received us with love, warmth and the assurance we were welcome.

153

What was it that "Poppy and Mommy" Myers were doing? They were taking heed to fulfill the ministry they had received from the Lord. They were given to hospitality (Romans 12:13), and they were faithful stewards of that gift by providing shelter for a Christian servant of the Lord.

There were times when Joyce and I seriously considered secular employment, so that we could have a place to call our own. But because of the faithfulness of saints like the Tharpes, the Bennetts and the Myers, we could continue to minister the Word of God. How abundantly the Lord has provided for all of us since then!

So very many Christians are under the false impression that unless they are working as full-time ministers, they have no ministry to the Lord. How very wrong they are! It is a major step in bold Bible living to seek the Lord in prayer for the present ministry He has called you to and then to fulfill it.

Some Christians don't realize that their ministry is their secular employment. It doesn't matter if your boss is not a Christian. The Bible says that we are to work, not to please men, but to please God: "...not with eyeservice, as menpleasers; but in singleness of heart, fearing God: And whatsoever ye do, do it heartily, as to the Lord, and not unto men; Knowing that of the Lord ye shall receive the reward of the inheritance: for ye serve the Lord Christ" (Colossians 3:22-24).

Christian! In your secular job you are serving the Lord Jesus Christ. As you type that letter, build that building, teach that child in school, it is the Lord Jesus that you are pleasing in your service.

Therefore, do not be as the world is, slothful in their work. Don't try to see how little actual work you can do in your alloted eight-hour day. Be a bold living Christian—"Work heartily as to the Lord!" In times like this, serving the Lord is very practical and down-to-earth. A bold Christian is punctual, shows respect to the boss, does his job without murmuring or disputing (Philippians 2:14), does not gossip with or about the other employees (Romans 1:29), trys to keep peace with all men (Hebrews 12:14).

In these days of disrespect and rebellion, this isn't always such an easy task. But it is part of your service to the Lord! It is the way that you will shine as lights of the world in the midst of a crooked and perverse nation (Philippians 2:15).

I know there are times when many Christians wish they could be doing something for the Lord that seems more "glamorous." Remember, the Bible says, "To everything there is a season, and a time to every purpose under the heaven" (Ecclesiastes 3:1). In the Lord's service, the most important thing is to know *His* purpose for your life, and then to walk in that purpose faithfully.

Often times, even when the Lord has a specific work for us to do, He has a timing that we may not understand. As we work in the job He has set before us, in obedience, He will reward us with greater things in accordance with His Word (Matthew 25:23). Remember that the Lord Jesus worked as a carpenter in unobtrusiveness for thirty years before He was sent out to fulfill His ministry. Moses was a simple shepherd on the backside of the desert for forty years before God used him as Israel's deliverer.

155

Perhaps my favorite biblical story of stewardship and its rewards is the one of Joseph in Genesis 39-41. As a slave in Potiphar's house, he was such an excellent steward that he was promoted over the entire household. Even when he reached the lowest of places—the prison—he was faithful to the Lord and to the prison warden. In due season, Joseph's faithfulness over the little things gained him the tremendous reward of ruling all of Egypt, second only to the Pharaoh himself!

If the Lord desires to use you in some place that seems lowly for a time, remember that a crucial part of bold Bible living is to have the courage to stand in the position that God has placed you, serving Him in obedience and love. For when you have been faithful in small things, even as Joseph was, God will place you as a ruler over many! It is a spiritual principle contained in His Word, and it cannot fail!

How to be a witness on the job

Part of faithful service to the Lord is to be a proper witness on the job. I received a question in the mail from an earnest Christian woman who was very unsure of herself. She wrote:

"I have often heard your broadcasts on bold Bible living. I have heard your challenges to witnessing for Christ. I am a Christian, but I am shy and not a good conversationalist. Does God expect me to be as good a witness as those who are blessed with the gift of speech?"

For this reader and all those who might ask the same question, here is my answer. There are many ways to witness for Christ, and vocal witnessing is only one of them. What you are and the way you conduct yourself is often more important than what you say. There are times that words are soon forgotten, but a Christian attitude will be long remembered by those who behold it. When you are sincerely helpful to your workmates on the job, when you refuse the temptation to join in their complaints, when you pray for their sick loved ones or give up a coffee break to listen to their problems, you have shown them the Lord Jesus Christ. Your dedicated, consecrated life can be a solid witness for the Lord in a hundred ways.

However, I don't think you should rule out the fact that you can speak for Christ, too. I'm in full sympathy with your feeling of not being able to speak effectively. For years, I was weighed down by an inability to speak freely. I stammered and stuttered so much that my father laughed at me when I first told him of my call to preach the Gospel.

However, during this time, three great scriptures helped me, and they have continued to help me through the years. I have now preached over 6,000 sermons and have spoken over the radio for twenty-eight years. I am humbly grateful for what the Word of God has brought to pass in my life. I'm sure these scriptures from His Word will help you as well.

(1) "Now therefore go, and I will be with thy mouth, and teach thee what thou shalt say" (Exodus 4:12). I didn't know this was God's promise given to Moses. I just came across it in my Bible, and I took it for my own life. God told me to "go" and He would be with my mouth. I really needed that. My mouth was not prone to speak smoothly, so to know I had God with my mouth was precious to me. Praise the Lord,

this truth helped me to begin preaching and speaking publicly for Christ everywhere.

(2) "The Spirit of the Lord spake by me, and his word was in my tongue" (2 Samuel 23:2). This was David's testimony, but I took it also for myself. I knew it was the help of the Spirit I needed, that the Spirit would use that Word in my tongue. "The Word in my tongue" meant to me that I should memorize much Scripture, so the Spirit could use it. For this reason I have led hundreds of other Christians in memorizing the great Bible passages. This is indeed one of the greatest favors I've ever been permitted to do for others—to stir them up to memorize God's holy Word.

(3) "Lord...grant unto thy servants, that with all boldness we may speak thy word, by stretching forth thine hand to heal; and that signs and wonders may be done by the name of Jesus" (Acts 4:29). This was the prayer of the early Christians, that God would grant them boldness to speak His Word. How many times I have made this my prayer, and blessed be God, He yet answers that prayer for boldness to speak His Word.

Doing your best is more important than being best!

A champion Christian gymnast participated in the Munich Olympics. After failing to win the coveted gold medal, she went into the stands to join her parents. Her mother shared with her these profound words of wisdom: "You've done your best, so you have nothing to regret," her mother advised. "Doing your best is more important than being the best."

These words have ministered to my heart. They are a perfect description of biblical stewardship. I know I may not be the best radio broadcaster. But I have done my best to fulfill my ministry. The Lord has been pleased and put me on the air into 89 different nations of the world.

Perhaps you are not the best intercessor. But doing your best in prayer is so much more important than not praying at all. When God has laid a task before you, or given you a job to perform, remember that it is your best that counts, and that it is His strength that will enable you to do it.

I learned this as a young man when I accepted an invitation to be editor of a national Gospel magazine. I succeeded a man who was a professional photographer.

I had never operated a press camera in my life. Soon, one was purchased for me—a Speed Graphic press camera. I read the basic instructions, experimented with a few pictures, then was ready to give up in despair when I saw the results. But the Holy Spirit reminded me of my testimony! "I can do all things through Christ which strengtheneth me" (Philippians 4:13).

Do you think that Jesus Christ does not know how to run a press camera? Or to preach a sermon, or to accomplish any other task that may ever come your way in His service? Of course, He can!

So when I would go to the great campaigns where I would take flash shots of the events, I fortified myself with a dozen affirmations of this truth: "I can do all things through Christ. I can operate this camera efficiently. I can, through Christ, take excellent pictures. I can do it, I can do it!"

In the five years I served with that ministry, I took many hundreds of pictures to be reproduced in magazines and books. While I never achieved any great heights as a photographer, my pictures were sharp and readily publishable.

Knowing my own limitations and failures in early attempts, I had no reason for pride about my attainments in the field of photography. I give Christ the honor and praise. I know it was through His ability that I was able to do my best. Impossibilities become realities when you live by this truth: I can do all things *through Christ!*

So whatever the task the Lord lays before you, whatever possessions, large or small, that He places in your hands, be faithful! Be a faithful steward in the small things, and God will use you greatly over many!

HOW TO BE USED OF GOD

1. It is in the heart of every Christian to be used of God. There is much work to be done, and the Lord of the harvest is calling for laborers. First, we must have a sure knowledge of our own salvation. We are witnesses for the Lord, "I know whom I have believed" (2 Timothy 1:12). "This is the record, that God hath given to us eternal life" (1 John 5:11). "The Spirit itself beareth witness with our spirit, that we are the children of God" (Romans 8:16).

2. We must have a working knowledge of the Bible. The Word alone reveals the plan of God for this life and eternity. By the Word we know about prayer, about healing, about giving, about walking with the Lord, about heaven and hell.

3. We need to be filled with the Spirit. Then we must be led by the Holy Spirit. Only the Spirit can anoint us for truly effective service.

4. We must have a heart of genuine love for others. Only the love of Christ can constrain us to be used of God. It was love that compelled Jesus to come, to heal, then to die for us. Now through His love we are to live for others.

5. We must know and practice the marvelous power of prayer. God promises to do amazing things in answer to Bible praying. We must invest

our money in the Lord's work. Our money is a part of our lives. Bountiful, liberal, cheerful giving always pleases God.

6. We must be bold and fearless. "The righteous are bold as a lion" (Proverbs 28:1). It was boldness for which the early Christians prayed so earnestly (Acts 4:29). The Lord will give us this holy boldness, which means confidence, courage, fearlessness and daring. We must explicitly obey the Lord's Word. "Go ye into all the world, and preach the gospel to every creature.... These signs shall follow them that believe; In my name shall they cast out devils...they shall lay hands on the sick, and they shall recover" (Mark 16:15, 17-18). Dare to carry out His orders!

7. To be used of God we must seek to bring glory and honor to Him. How? Yield yourself to the Lord right now. Pray, "Here I am, Lord, ready to be used of thee!" Yield your all to the Lord. Then ask as Paul did, "Lord, what wilt thou have me to do?" (Acts 9:6). Review these essentials often. Set out to be used of God!

Chapter 13

THEY *SHALL* RECOVER

Delmar Kingsriter is a missionary to Malawi, Africa, where he has served the Lord for many years. He shared this amazing experience of how we can boldly employ the mighty spiritual weapons the Lord has given us to live in divine health. This is a testimony of bold Bible living across the world.

"They shall take up serpents; and if they drink any deadly thing, it shall not hurt them; they shall lay hands on the sick, and *they shall recover*" (Mark 16:18).

"This certainly must be a favorite scripture for many missionaries," Delmar began. "It certainly is mine, for it provides me both defensive and offensive weapons for divine health. Satan is well aware of the devastating results when the prayer of faith is offered for the sick.

"Since the time of Christ, the healing of the sick has been the most potent weapon in the hands of God's servants. Therefore, Satan often seeks to destroy those who are carrying the message of deliverance from sin and sickness. There have been many occasions when

I've had to quote and claim this scripture when satanic powers were seeking to destroy my very existence.

"I recall one occasion when a missionary family, together with myself, my wife and my children, traveled by boat to a remote village in Africa. The Gospel had first penetrated this village only a few weeks before, and we were seeing wonderful success.

"After a glorious meeting, crowned by a water baptismal service, we had just begun the three hour journey back to our base camp when a huge swarm of poisonous African bees attacked us. Before we were able to find shelter in a smoke-filled hut, each of us had sustained as many as fifty to seventy-five stings, mostly around the face and head. I realized we were in danger of losing our lives, for many people have died after being stung only a few times.

"Within moments, the wife of the other missionary became desperately ill and collapsed in the dust. It was in that instant that this scripture became very precious to me and seemed to be the last thread of hope between life and death. None of us present that day can ever doubt the power of the Word of God. We gathered around this still form and quietly quoted this scripture, 'They shall take up serpents; and if they drink any deadly thing, it shall not hurt them; they shall lay hands on the sick, and they shall recover.' Then we offered a simple, but desperate, plea for help to the only One who *could* help us in that hour—the Lord Jesus Christ.

"Within a few seconds, color came back into the face of that missionary's wife, and she stood up and said, 'I am well.' All the way back to the camp, our little children joined us in worshiping the Lord for a mighty deliverance. There was not a sign on any of us of the swelling that usually accompanies the stings of even the less poisonous honey bee.

"This was a modern-day deliverance, not unlike that of the three Hebrew children who God delivered from the fiery furnace. Is it any wonder this scripture verse has become one of my favorites?"

Most people would agree that health is a universal word. Those who have lost it desire it above everything else. Those who have it employ every means to maintain it.

It is obvious from God's Word that He has a great deal to say about health. My firm conviction is that if we gave more attention to the clear provisions which God makes for healthy bodies through our Lord Jesus Christ, we would be living a fuller, more victorious Christian life than we had ever dreamed. It would be a life of bold Bible living that would attract the unsaved of the world to our doorsteps to obtain the same thing!

Because there are some very common and often-asked questions regarding healing that I receive from mail all over the world, I would like to answer several of them. Perhaps you have asked some of these questions yourself, or know a friend that needs these answers. I pray they would be a blessing to further your bold Bible walk.

"I have received prayer for my healing. What must I do now?"

After you have had prayer for your healing, my challenge to you is to do what the Word says, act on its promises. First of all, the Bible promises us, "with His stripes we are healed" (Isaiah 53:5). Affirm what God says about your healing. Make it personal and declare, "By His stripes *I* am healed." Then begin to thank and praise the Lord for healing you, for praise is the language of faith.

One night before a Crusade service, I was invited to accompany the pastor of the church where I was ministering. We went to the home of a man who had been completely bedfast for eighteen months with a paralytic stroke. Since the message of divine healing was comparatively new to this man, I explained to him the truth of Mark 16:17-18 where Jesus said, "These signs shall follow them that believe.... they shall lay hands on the sick, and they shall recover."

I said to the man, "Not everyone for whom we pray is healed instantly. But as surely as you take this verse from Jesus Christ in faith and hold fast to it without wavering, he says you shall recover. It may be instantly, it may be a matter of hours or days. But this is a positive statement, 'You *shall* recover!'"

This man received the truth with an open mind and heart and assured me of his confidence in Christ's ability to make the Word real in his life. The pastor and I laid hands on him in the name of Jesus and prayed for his healing. Although there were no immediate visible results, this man was not dismayed. He was trustful that the Lord would perform His promise. We had given him the basis for healing, "with His stripes we are healed." He realized that the *finished work of Christ* gives us provision for healing, but our *faith* must produce the full benefit of it in our lives.

I had noticed a large hall clock just adjacent to the

bedroom door that always chimed on the hour. So we asked the man to make a bold affirmation of faith every time he heard the hall clock chime that another hour of the day or night had passed. The paralytic man agreed that he would look up every time he heard the clock chime the hour, and he would say, "Thank You, Jesus, by Your stripes I am healed."

The paralytic stroke had left this man's fingers drawn up, his face and mouth disfigured and turned to one side, and his legs drawn. So it was with real effort that he began to exclaim triumphantly, "Thank You, Jesus, by Your stripes I am healed."

This all happened on a Monday night. I left to go back to my home that same evening. On Thursday morning, however, this is what happened as the pastor reported it to me.

Our paralytic friend called him on the phone, "Come out, Pastor, I have something wonderful I want to share with you." The pastor went to the home, and there he witnessed a mighty miracle. This same man that had been virtually a prisoner to his bed of suffering stood in the living room smiling and declaring, "It has worked just like Brother Gossett assured me! I have praised in faith, 'Thank You, Jesus, by Your stripes I am healed.' And the Lord has healed me!" The man's fingers were straightened out, his legs were normal, the disfigurement of the mouth and face were all gone. He was completely healed of the paralytic stroke!

I relate this miraculous account that you may realize the importance of rising up with a new testimony that harmonizes with the Word of God. Hold fast to that testimony boldly without wavering.

God, who has given His Word, will watch over that Word to perform it.

This is a challenge of utmost importance to you. Begin to say, "Thank You, Jesus, by Your stripes I am healed." Believe it from your heart. See Christ bearing in His own body your infirmities and diseases. Then realize that through the bleeding stripes He endured, He provided healing for you. Now repeat from a full heart, "Thank You, Jesus, by Your stripes I am healed." These are not magic words. They are words that harmonize with God's Word, and God watches over His Word to really make it good. I believe it will happen in your behalf!

"I just don't feel any different, even though I have been prayed for."

Well, beloved, this is perhaps the greatest pitfall in healing that we ever meet. Feeling is not faith. Your feelings will deceive you. When you are prayed for according to the Bible, some people do feel differently. But faith in God accepts the healing regardless of feelings, knowing that God cannot lie. He promises, "I am the Lord that healeth thee" (Exodus 15:26). Whether you feel God's power in your body or not, the whole matter rests with His Word. Jesus said, "They shall lay hands on the sick, and they *shall* recover" (Mark 16:18). And "He sent his word, and *healed them*" (Psalm 107:20). All healing is based on the authority of the Word. Christ healed the sick and cast out spirits with His own Word.

There is a remarkable testimony that confirms the power in the above scripture from Mark's Gospel.

I know of a woman whose doctors had pronounced

her incurably ill. She made many attempts to receive her healing, going again and again for prayer. But after many months she only grew worse and became discouraged. Then she heard our Bold Bible Living broadcast on the scripture from Mark, chapter sixteen.

The truth "They shall lay hands on the sick, and they shall recover" challenged her. She realized that it wasn't in the many prayers of others that she would be healed but by steadfastly believing this promise of Jesus and acting accordingly.

Friends tried to discourage her, even as she maintained her new confession. "How are you feeling?" they would inquire. "You're not looking well at all," they would add, sympathetically.

"I'm not going on how I look or feel," she would answer, refusing to waver in her faith. "Jesus said, 'They shall lay hands on the sick, and they shall recover,' and that's for me. I have had hands laid on me for my healing. I know I am recovering."

These "Job-comforters," her so-called "well-wishers," persisted in trying to throw cold water on her fervent confession.

But she was resolute. She had had hands laid upon her body and now she expected the Lord to be faithful. She would not dishonor Him by disbelieving His promises. This was His Word to her, she reflected, and God was not a man that He should lie (Numbers 23:19). Her part in this drama of faith was to hold fast to her confession without wavering (Hebrews 10:23).

It was a good fight of faith she fought. The Lord made her completely whole! Believe His Word. Make it your testimony! Act boldly upon it! And you too will know the truth, "He sent His word, and healed them."

I don't seem to have the faith. I guess I won't be healed.

Listen, beloved, if you are a Christian, you do have the faith. God has given to every one of His children the measure of faith (Romans 12:3). *Use* that faith! Put it into action! You will be made whole! Declare assuredly, "I do have faith! I do believe!"

You ask, "Well, how can I strengthen my faith?" The Bible says, "faith comes by hearing the Word of God." Study, soak in God's Word. Accept the glorious promises at face value and act boldly accordingly!

"What if old symptoms of the affliction I had return?"

Recognize it is a trick of Satan. Refuse to have them; "Resist the devil, and he will flee from you" (James 4:7).

Just a couple of years ago, I awakened one morning with a splitting headache—literally. The pain was so severe it seemed that the back left side of my skull was splitting off from the rest of my head—and those pains began to reoccur almost daily. It was very unusual for me because head pains were something I had never experienced in my life.

The headaches reached a climax in severity the following month on February 16th, while Joyce and I were at a Crusade. I determined then that I must meet with the Lord in prayer, praise and the confession of His Word.

The Bible prophesies, "And it shall come to pass in the last days, saith God, I will pour out of my Spirit upon all flesh: and your sons and your daughters shall

170

prophesy, and your young men shall see visions, and your old men shall dream dreams" (Acts 2:17). In the early morning of February 17th, as I lay on my bed confessing, "by His stripes I am healed," I had an unusual experience.

I saw a man come towards me and lay his hand on the back of my head. A warm, penetrating oil flowed into the "split" there and ministered healing, taking away all the pain. To the best of my knowledge, these are the words I spoke, "Sir, you must be the Apostle Paul," which was a strange statement to make. But then he replied, "I am an angel of the Lord." Hebrews 1:13-14 declares that angels are ministering spirits sent forth to minister to the heirs of salvation!

When I returned to a state of complete awareness, all of the pain was gone!

I told Joyce about the experience and, a little later, I shared it with the ministering brethren at the Crusade. Everyone rejoiced with me at the Lord's goodness!

But unexpectedly, when we returned home the next week, the heavy pains in my head returned. I was somewhat dismayed at the return of the pain, until suddenly I realized that the headaches were actually lying symptoms and not the real physical pains at all! Jesus had already provided healing; it was *His Word* that I had confessed when the healing was manifested at the Crusade.

On the night I arrived at a Full Gospel Business-men's banquet in Arlington, Virginia, I had one more bout with the lying symptoms of headaches. I resisted them emphatically in Jesus' conquering name, and the pains left...never to return again!

In John 10:10 Jesus reveals that the devil is a thief that comes to steal, kill and destroy. The old thief sought to steal the healing the Lord had performed for me. But realizing the power of God's Word, I refused to accept anything that would destroy the reality of the healing work of Jesus. I praise the Lord I have not had a headache since, not even for a moment!

You have the right, as a believer, to defeat the devil in the all-powerful name of Jesus. The Bible tells us that we overcome or "come over" the devil by the blood of Jesus and the word of our testimony. Know the power of the blood. Know the authority of the Word in your testimony. Use them boldly!

12 BOLD STEPS TO YOUR HEALTH AND HAPPINESS

1. *Live close to the Lord Jesus Christ.* This is a place of security, as the multitudes discovered when Jesus walked the shores of Galilee. Those who heard Him, touched Him, or where touched by Him received healing in their bodies. He is "the same yesterday, and today, and for ever" (Hebrews 13:8), so dwelling close to Him still holds the key to our health.

2. *Claim the power and protection of the blood of Jesus.* Satan is defeated by the blood of the Lamb, and the word of our testimony (Revelation 12:11). The power of the blood sacrifice of Jesus Christ upon the cross is undiminished to this day. With the ever mounting forces of evil in the world today, it is most important to boldly claim the protective power of the blood of Jesus Christ.

3. *"Be ye filled with the Holy Ghost."* The born-again Christian becomes a new creature in Christ. Once you are born again, you can move one step further to your baptism in the Holy Spirit. This infilling of the Spirit will bring you power—power to overcome the enemy in the name of Jesus Christ. "But if the Spirit of him that raised up Jesus from the dead dwell in you, he that raised up Christ from the dead shall also quicken your mortal bodies" (Romans 8:11).

4. *Study God's Word daily.* "In the beginning was the Word. . . . in him was life" (John 1:1,4). There is life in the Word, and the reading of the Word gives health to all that find them (Proverbs 4:20-22). We must remain in the words of God daily, for they are a lamp to our feet, and a light to our path (Psalm 119:105).

5. *Do not neglect the rules of health.* Since our bodies are the temple of the Holy Spirit (1 Corinthians 6:19), we should not defile that temple. We should do our best to get proper amounts of sleep and to eat nutritious foods. We should not allow ourselves to become overweight. Proper exercise is necessary to keep our bodies strong, and we should not defile our bodies with toxic agents such as alcohol, drugs and tobacco.

6. *Stay in Christian fellowship.* When the Christian wanders from Christian fellowship and increasingly associates with the world, his spiritual life becomes dulled, and he becomes subject to the temptations and illnesses of the world. Jesus told us to seek first the Kingdom of God and His righteousness. When we find this Kingdom through being born again, we should not turn about and seek the kingdom of the world again. To do so is destructive to our souls and body health.

7. *Speak in a heavenly language.* This applies in two ways to the Spirit-filled Christian. First of all, the Christian can speak words of love and

peace, rather than words that are rude or accusatory. Jesus said, "But those things which proceed out of the mouth come forth from the heart; and they defile the man" (Matthew 15:18). Instead of speaking words of defilement, a Christian can speak words of health and wholeness. "A wholesome tongue is a tree of life" (Proverbs 15:4).

Then, the Spirit-baptized Christian can also speak in his new tongue, the prayer language he was given through the baptism in the Holy Spirit. The Bible says that speaking in tongues edifies us, it builds us up (1 Corinthians 14:4). You can be built up spiritually, and therefore be affected physically, when you faithfully pray in your prayer language every day.

8. *Maintain a good conscience.* This is necessary for good health. Any sense of guilt, whether repressed or active in our thoughts, is destructive to our wholeness. If we live a holy life, not subjecting ourselves to evil which produces guilt, we shall find ourselves living in wholeness and health.

9. *Do not fail to give to your church and to those in need.* The spirit of miserliness can be very damaging to your spirit and to your body. Many otherwise good Christians completely destroy their wholeness by being unwilling to share freely of their substance with their church and with those who are in need. Giving to others produces happiness within our hearts, and this produces a

sense of well-being, joy and health.

10. *Do not cease to be joyful.* On the day of Pentecost, those who were in the upper room were so joyful and wonderously full of the Spirit that some thought them to be drunk. Praising God has a power that releases our spirits and sets us free. Often praise itself has brought healing to many who have been afflicted. Living and being free in the Spirit produces health.

11. *If you become ill, ask for prayer.* There is no disgrace in becoming ill. It's what we do about it that counts. If we feel sorry for ourselves, become disgruntled or morose, we are dishonoring our heavenly Father whose delight is to see us in good health. The Scriptures are clear that we are to call on the elders to anoint us with oil and pray for us (James 5:14-15), or to ask another believer to lay hands on us and pray (Mark 16:18). The exercise of spiritual compassion has a healing effect both on those who are prayed for and those who pray.

12. *Remember, above all, that what you say is what you get!* Confess the health that you have in Jesus Christ daily. Remember always that with His stripes you were healed nearly two thousand years ago. When you are ill, "hold fast to that confession of faith without wavering." God is good to His Word. He has upheld it even above His name (Psalm 138:2). He hastens His Word to

perform it! (Jeremiah 1:12). So, boldly confess health in the name of Jesus Christ, and it will be yours!

THERE'S NO ROOM FOR GLOOM...

Chapter 14

A SMILE IS MY STYLE

At the end of the opening service of a recent crusade I was conducting, a man cornered me.

"Now, Brother Gossett, before I decide whether I will be back to hear you preach each night," the man announced, "I must know what your doctrine is. Tell me now, what is your doctrine?"

As the man looked at me intently, I felt an uneasiness as I sought to answer his inquiry about "my doctrine."

"You want to know my doctrine, is that it?" I asked, stalling for a few moments to know how to give him the right answer.

"Yes, sir," he shot back. "It's very important to me that I listen to sound doctrine only. So I must know what your doctrine is."

There was no evidence of any smile on his face, nor in his eyes. I felt quite on the spot.

"Well, brother," I replied. "Among other things, I believe in the doctrine of smiling."

"The doctrine of smiling," he instantly responded. "I never heard of that doctrine!"

"You may not call it a doctrine," I answered, "but it's a good Bible teaching that the Lord wants us to smile, and smile often."

"Did you ever read this scripture?" I asked him. 'Rejoice, because your names are written in heaven' (Luke 10:20). There are many commands in the Bible that tell us to rejoice. I don't see how one can rejoice without smiling. A smiling Christian is a good advertisement for the grace of Jesus."

"I believe many other things," I concluded. "But I believe in the 'doctrine of smiling.' Smiling fills one of the prime requirements of looking like a Christian."

"But let all those that put their trust in thee rejoice: let them ever shout for joy, because thou defendest them: let them also that love thy name be joyful in thee" (Psalm 5:11).

Joy is the attractive force in bold Bible living. It is the best advertisement to a world that has an abundance of sorrow and woes. The phrase "joy-unspeakable" (1 Peter 1:8) is more than just a high sounding phrase; it is to be the experience of every child of God...unspeakable joy in Christ (John 15:11).

One woman in Seattle was of the persuasion that to look like a Christian required a long face like a "Missouri mule." It seemed that her conviction was that it was almost a sin to smile.

One day she was out in her yard doing some yard work. A man pushing a junk cart came down her street. He was collecting old beer bottles that day.

Seeing this particular woman in her yard, he called out to her, "Lady, do you have any beer bottles at your

182

house? I'm collecting old beer bottles."

The woman was highly offended at the inference that she would have beer bottles in her house. Stiffly, with an angered look on her countenance, she walked over to the front of her yard.

Peering across the picket fence, she shook her bony finger at the junk dealer, "Do I look like a person who would have beer bottles in my house?"

The fellow took a long look at her scowling face, then turned back to his cart. As he got a firm hold on it, he looked at her again.

"By the way," he inquired, "do you have any old vinegar bottles at your house?"

For the truly born-again, bold living Christian, a genuine smile is always in style. We should affirm it often, "A smile is my style."

The Bible declares, "A merry heart doeth good like a medicine" (Proverbs 17:22). "He that is of a merry heart hath a continual feast" (Proverbs 15:15). The cause of a cheerful countenance is a merry heart.

Remember, each day of your life there are many reasons to praise the Lord and be joyful. You can smile at the day, for "This is the day which the Lord hath made; we will rejoice and be glad in it" (Psalm 118:24). You can thank the Lord for how He has chosen to make you, for you are "fearfully and wonderfully made" (Psalm 139:14).Or you can just obey the Bible which abounds with commands to sing, to shout, to rejoice, "Sing, O daughter of Zion; shout, O Israel; be glad and rejoice with all the heart, O daughter of Jerusalem" (Zephaniah 3:14).

A Christian man in Kansas City was busy passing

out Gospel tracts on the streets to all passersby. While he was an earnest, dedicated Christian, he had forgotten the importance of Christian joy, the grace of smiling. To him, evangelism was all dead serious business to warn people of their need of Christ.

As he thrust this tract into the hand of a businessman, the businessman noticed the title of the tract: *"Why You Should Become a Christian."* He studied the title for a few moments, then looked at the Christian. He noticed his sad face, his expression of woefulness, the lack of sparkle in his eyes.

Handing the tract back to the Christian man, he stated, "Thank you for offering me this tract. But I've got enough troubles of my own!"

Being fishers of men should be done by those who know this word, "Be glad in the Lord, and rejoice, ye righteous: and shout for joy, all ye that are upright in heart" (Psalm 32:11).

In my own years of evangelism, I have definitely observed that joy is the real secret to winning souls. In our meetings, I've noticed that it is the joyful, living testimony that stirs the people. It is the person who is so full of joy that he can hardly speak, as the tears stream down his face, that moves the people, that touches their hearts.

When we speak the Word with assurance and joy, it brings conviction to the listeners. When the Word becomes more real to you than any word man has ever spoken, your lips will be filled with laughter, your heart will be filled with joy, and you will have a victorious Christian life.

How many times I have seen that the hesitant testimony is a forerunner of failure, and the joyful testimony is a forerunner of victory.

Christians are only as strong as they are filled with the joy of the Lord. A church is only as strong and influential for Christ in a community as it is filled with the real joy of the Lord.

Why? Because "The joy of the Lord is your strength" (Nehemiah 8:10). When people complain of lacking strength, or talk about how weak they are, often their real lack is the joy of the Lord.

When the Israelites returned from Babylon to rebuild the walls of Jerusalem, Nehemiah found many of them were mourning and weeping; some were suffering with diseases; others were weak and undernourished. Not a few were downcast, defeated and despondent. When Nehemiah asked God's help for His people, God gave them this message: "This day is holy unto the Lord your God; mourn not, nor weep. . . . neither be ye sorry; for the joy of the Lord is your strength" (Nehemiah 8:9-10).

"The joy of the Lord is your strength!" This was God's answer for Israel then; it is God's answer for us today.

The joy of the Lord is not just a side-product of our Christian walk. It is both the strength that keeps us living boldly for God and the result of moving boldly in His name. It is within us all of the time, if we are willing to receive it and walk in it.

Jesus is the joy of living. He brought to the world a life of joy. On the night of His birth, the angel announced the "good tidings of great joy, which shall be to all people. For unto you is born this day in the city of David a Savior, which is Christ the Lord" (Luke 2:10-11).

Wherever Jesus went throughout His earthly life, He brought joy to the sorrowing, cheer to the downcast, and gladness to those who were sitting in the shadows of death. One aim of His earthly ministry was to restore joy to human hearts which had been languishing in the shackles of sin and sadness.

In bold Bible living we "rejoice with joy unspeakable and full of glory" (1 Peter 1:8). Jesus is our reason for rejoicing—more than that, He is our Source of joy.

Some time ago, I read these remarkable paragraphs, and I want to pass them on to you. In answer to the question: Where is happiness? the author answers:

Not in Unbelief—Voltaire was an infidel of the most pronounced type. He wrote: "I wish I had never been born."

Not in Pleasure—Lord Byron lived a life of pleasure, if anyone did. He wrote: "The worm, the canker, the grief are mine alone."

Not in Money—Jay Gould, the American millionaire, had plenty of money. When dying, he said, "I suppose I am the most miserable man on earth."

Not in Position and Fame—Lord Beaconsfield enjoyed more than his share of both. He wrote: "Youth is a mistake; manhood a struggle; old age a regret."

Not in Military Glory—Alexander the Great conquered the known world of his day. Having done so, he wept in his tent, because he said, "There are no more worlds to conquer."

Where then is happiness and joy found?

The answer is simple: in Christ alone. Jesus said, "I will see you again, and your heart shall rejoice, and your joy no man taketh from you" (John 16:22).

Jesus gives us joy, joy unspeakable—not only shall we have it in heaven, but right here in this present world, we have abounding joy!

Losing the joy

One of the greatest tragedies is that Christians sometimes lose their joy. Definite acts of sin (compare 2 Samuel 12 and Psalm 51), as well as careless drifting from the Lord, are causes for losing this bold joy in the Lord.

While losing our joy is a tragedy, there is a great assurance in the Bible that it can be found again. When David was convicted of his sin with Bathsheba he cried, "Wash me thoroughly from mine iniquity, and cleanse me from my sin." After that he prayed, "Lord, restore unto me the joy of thy salvation" (Psalm 51:2, 12). And the joy of the Lord was restored to him.

If you are one who has lost his joy in the Lord, go before God in heart-searching. Confess every sin unto Him. Ask Him as David did, "Restore unto me the joy of thy salvation." The Lord will surely do it!

We are living in days when barrenness of soul and depression characterizes many. If you are an unbeliever who lacks this joy today, you can have it by coming to Jesus Christ. As Isaiah 12:3 says, "Therefore with joy shall ye draw water out of the wells of salvation."

Or if you, as a backslider, have lost that vital life of bold joy through drifting, make it your prayer, "O Lord, wilt thou not revive us again: that thy people may rejoice in thee?" (Psalm 85:6). Closeness of fellowship with Christ restores that joy.

It is very important that we keep joy-filled. By a bold, joy-filled life we can be of greater service to others in addition to the personal profit that is ours. Remember, a joy-filled life is the best advertisement for the Gospel.

The joy-filled life is contagious. It is very attractive in this world of sorrow, disappointment and heartbreak.

Thank God for the joy-filled life!

THERE'S NO ROOM FOR GLOOM

"This is the day which the Lord hath made; we will rejoice and be glad in it" (Psalm 118:24).

FIRST: The Lord makes each new day for us. Whatever God makes is good, and good for us. "And God saw every thing that he had made, and, behold, it was very good" (Genesis 1:31). Since the Lord made the day, it's a day for joyful good living, not ill-living.

SECOND: God made the day; He expects us to rejoice and be glad. "Serve the Lord with gladness" not sadness commands Psalm 100. Say these words, "The Lord made this day for me. I shall be glad and rejoice!"

THIRD: With God *for* me, and *within* me, there's absolutely no room for gloom! God isn't a gloomy God, and He doesn't want gloomy children!

FOURTH: The Bible commands us, "Neither give place to the devil" (Ephesians 4:27). When you give place for gloom in your life, you are giving place to the devil. He is the author of gloom.

FIFTH: Make it your glad declaration: In my life, *there's no room for gloom!* Hallelujah!

SIXTH: So many of God's children are in low

spirits. They are depressed, mopish, disgusted with life. Here is the positive bold living way to lift yourself out of the doldrums: Make no more room for gloom by being glad and rejoicing in the Lord . . . always!

SEVENTH: Right now walk out of your slough of despondency. Put a sudden stop to sulking! Life has much to dampen the spirit. But you are partaking in bold Bible living; you are living by God's Word! Do not sink to the level of the pessimistic crowd. Quit wearing that long face. Your Lord is alive! He is risen! Hallelujah!

EIGHTH: Be a sparkling, bold, joyful person. Praise the Lord often. Count your blessings at bedtime, and you will be amazed at all the Lord has done!

NINTH: Tune your ear with me now to a personal message from our God: "Fear thou not, for I am with thee: be not dismayed; for I am thy God: I will strengthen thee; yea, I will help thee; yea, I will uphold thee with the right hand of my righteousness (Isaiah 41:10). How can you be down when God is holding you up? No more room for joyless, dismal living . . . He is our God!

TENTH: Congratulations, bold conqueror! There's no more room for gloom!

Chapter 15

THE VICTORY OF SONG

The story is told of a Glasgow woman one night gazing reflectively into the murky waters of the River Clyde. The darkness of the night seemed to press down into her very soul. The black, deep river reminded her of the ugliness of her own life of sin.

As she stood at the foot of the ferry steps, she was suddenly gripped by a desire to plunge into the river and end her bitter life. But she trembled as she heard a clear strong voice from above singing, "There is a fountain filled with Blood."

She listened, spellbound. She would wait, she decided, until the song was finished. Another voice joined in, and the words of the next stanza rushed into her heart with a new hope:

"The dying thief rejoiced to see
that fountain in his day;
And there may I, though vile as he,
wash all my sins away."

Gripped by this message, the woman dashed up the ferry steps to ask the singers if this One about whom they were singing could help her. Eagerly she listened as they pointed her to Christ. The woman's wasted life was changed to a fruitful life of service to the Lord.

This woman became a successful servant of God in the slums of Glasgow. God had worked through a song of testimony to reach this destitute soul, and in turn she was converted and used of the Lord to help the lost find peace, forgiveness and victory in Jesus.

Truly singing the praise and testimony of God is one of our instruments of power! Thank God for the beautiful inspiration and the spiritual liberation of Christian singing. There is victory in song!

"Let the saints be joyful ... let them sing aloud upon their beds. Let the high praises of God be in their mouth, and a two-edged sword in their hand" (Psalm 149:5-6).

This is real bold Bible living ... to cultivate the singing heart!

The world has perverted song to purposes of evil passion. Such songs become one of the most alluring agencies of temptation. But when we are converted, the Lord does some wonderful things for us.

"He brought me up also out of a horrible pit, out of the miry clay, and set my feet upon a rock, and established my goings. And he hath put a *new song* in my mouth, even praise unto our God: many shall see it, and fear, and shall trust in the Lord" (Psalm 40:2-3).

I can hardly emphasize enough the great victory there is in song, in singing the praises of the Lord. There is a real release and therapy in singing songs of spiritual liberation, songs of testimony, songs about the Lord's power and keeping.

As David said, "The Lord hath put a new song in my mouth, even praise unto our God." Second

Chronicles 29:30 says, "And they sang praises with gladness, and . . . they worshipped."

In the book of Ezra it describes how the people sang and praised the Lord with great joy. This gladness and joy in their singing and praising was their strength. From this singing they derived spiritual and mental health to rebuild the temple and the city of Jerusalem! Indeed they were strong and confident because of the song in their mouths!

Heartfelt singing is charged with divine power. There is victory in song!

There are two primary secrets to maintaining a singing heart: (1) Be full of the Word; (2) Be full of the Spirit.

(1) "Let the word of Christ dwell in you richly in all wisdom; teaching and admonishing one another in psalms and hymns and spiritual songs, singing with grace in your hearts to the Lord" (Colossians 3:16).

When you are full of the Word, it produces a bold, glad song. Confessing the Word aloud will bring forth an anthem of praise.

When troubles come, learn to go at them with song. When griefs arise, sing them down. Praise God by singing; that will lift you above trials of every sort.

I remember a time when I faced a very severe test. It seemed that it would crush my spirit and bring me to frustrating defeat. The need was a financial one; I was going to lose my car by repossession.

I boldly began to affirm, "My God shall supply all my need according to his riches in glory by Christ Jesus" (Philippians 4:19). I kept it up for about fifteen minutes, confessing it aloud over and over again. In time, that became a real song in my mouth and in my heart!

I resisted the temptation to doubt by singing praises unto God. As I held my heart steady by singing, the Lord worked miraculously on our behalf and supplied the need!

Being full of the Word will cause you to "sing with grace in your heart to the Lord."

(2) Being filled with the Spirit will also produce a singing heart. Ephesians 5:18-20 says, "Be not drunk with wine, wherein is excess; but be filled with the Spirit; speaking to yourselves in psalms and hymns and spiritual songs, singing and making melody in your heart to the Lord; giving thanks always for all things unto God and the Father in the name of our Lord Jesus Christ."

The Spirit-filled life, lived in the bold radiance of the Spirit, is wonderful! "I will sing with the spirit, and I will sing with the understanding also" (1 Corinthians 14:15). When you are controlled by the Spirit, He invariably inspires much song from your heart.

Every great move of the Spirit in past history was characterized by bold, gallant singing. What did Israel do when God delivered them from Egypt with a mighty hand? "Then sang Moses and the children of Israel this song unto the Lord. . . . The Lord is my strength and song, and he is become my salvation . . . I will exalt him" (Exodus 15:1-2).

What produced one of the most unusual interventions of God in the New Testament? "And at midnight Paul and Silas prayed, and sang praises unto God. . . . And suddenly there was a great earthquake, so that the foundations of the prisons were shaken: and immediately all the doors were opened, and every one's bands were loosed" (Acts 16:25-26).

Our circumstances may be dismal at times, and we may deplore the troubles besetting us, but our difficulties are usually mild compared to Paul and Silas. Their backs had been beaten to ribbons; they were thrust in that dirty, dark, inner dungeon with their feet fast in the stocks.

However, these men were the righteous of the Lord—"as bold as a lion"—who could sing praises to God even under such circumstances. God intervened for them and He will intervene for us if we demonstrate such loving confidence and bold faith in our God...to praise Him in song, even when everything around us cries out, "Defeat!"

There is no defeat to the bold living Christian who knows this song, "Thanks be unto God, which always causeth us to triumph in Christ" (2 Corinthians 2:14).

"Serve the Lord with gladness: come before his presence with singing" (Psalm 100:2).

God delights in your song unto Him! Whether you have talent to sing or not, you are singing best when it is unto the Lord! Such song has wonderful power...power to banish gloom, to quicken your spirit, to inspire you to bold courage for living in an age where God's way of life is being pushed aside by Satan.

In heaven we shall be a singing people. And here on earth we should keep our hearts drawn heavenward by singing.

Fill your home with song. Teach your children to sing. Sing as you travel to and from work, or as you work about the house. Songs of praise to Jesus can go with us wherever God leads us as we walk boldly in Him. Words in songs are words that work wonders!

I shall never forget my Saba experience years ago. Arriving on the small Dutch Antilles Island was a unique experience. Pastor Williams of the Wesleyan Holiness Church met us at the airport and took us immediately up a steep mountain that came winding down into several villages until we arrived at the capital city.

Ministering there in Saba was a delight. It was during a song service that the Holy Spirit spoke a clear word to me that has remained with me throughout my years of ministry. The Sabans were singing with inspiration:

> "And now, hallelujah,
> The rest of my days
> Shall gladly be spent
> In promoting His praise!"

The Spirit of God spoke to my heart: "That's your ministry. The rest of your days shall gladly be spent in promoting His praise!"

I say it unashamedly: I am a promoter of praise. And one of the most blessed ways I have found to give those praises is in the victory of song.

A friend of mine, R. C. Cunningham, wrote a beautiful description of the importance and all-inclusiveness of song:

"Songs of praise are an integral part of the Spirit-filled life 365 days of the year, not merely on any certain day.

"One of the best known songs of praise is the Great Doxology. One hymnologist said, 'It is doubtful if any stanza of religious poetry ever written has been so often, so universally, and so heartily sung in the worship of God as this.'

"The word 'doxology' means a short hymn full of direct praise to God. Examine it carefully and you will see there is great meaning and significance in every line.

"*Praise God from whom all blessings flow.* God is the fountain of everything that is good. 'Every good gift and every perfect gift is from above' (James 1:17). So if we want a blessing our gaze should be vertical rather than horizontal.

"*Praise Him, all creatures here below.* In the last half of Psalm 148 the Scripture summons the creatures of the sea, the lightnings, the mountains and forest, the beasts and the birds to unite with all ranks and ages of men and women to give homage and praise to their Creator. The purpose of all creation is to render praise to God, and this purpose eventually shall be filled. Blessed are they who do it here and now, voluntarily.

"*Praise Him above, ye heavenly host.* Not only the angels, but also the sun and moon, the heavens and all the stars of light, are called to participate in the doxology of the universe (Psalm 148:1-6). If the Psalmist were on earth today, he would include the satellites and space travelers, for these too will glorify the Lord.

"*Praise Father, Son, and Holy Ghost.* The Father loves us, the Son redeems us and the Spirit enlivens us. Surely we have abundant cause to praise the Holy Trinity!"

Have you lost your song?

Perhaps the songs we have been referring to have become clogged up in your life. Many times people allow the cares of the world to weigh them down.

A few years ago a large excavating job was being conducted in the Roman Forum. As the rubbish was being cleared away, suddenly there gushed forth the water of a spring that had been choked up for centuries. Once again the water of the stream flashed in the sunlight.

In the same way as this stream had been choked and hidden by the accumulation of rubbish, so many of you have allowed the spring of gladness and joyful song in your heart to be choked up.

There are many different things that can make up the rubbish heap in your life that keeps you from boldly singing with joy. Among them are unbelief, fear, the roots of bitterness that grow up, wrong attitudes, hatred, ill-will, avarice, anger. And the list always grows bigger—backbiting, jealousy, despondency, remorse, guilt.

Friend, you have been the devil's dumping ground for too long. I challenge you right now: rise up and have a rebellion against all these things. Get down to business and have a rubbish-clearing of everything that is choking up your spring of gladness and polluting your mind and body with real sicknesses, disabilities and weaknesses.

You cannot trifle with the Lord; His ways are best. Strike a blow for victory now! Bring yourself into harmony with God. Bold Bible living doesn't happen just by chance. You have to put yourself into this thing!

Get that rubbish cleared away by asking and receiving forgiveness from the Father through the name of Jesus Christ. Allow Jesus to become the

Master of your life. Then let that spring of gladness leap forth and shine in the sunlight of God's love!

When Hezekiah, the good king of Judah, cleaned up the house of the Lord and repaired the altar, the Bible tells us that then "the song of the Lord began."

Perhaps you have thought your life was confined to mournful, monotonous music. But God has some gay violins, cheery flutes and soothing harps for you to play. Get in tune with God! Harmonize with heaven! It may require some drastic action on your part to break the discords that you have played so long. But in good time you will break forth in a bright new tune that will be pleasing to God, will give a lift to your life and will begin to inspire others to change their tune!

"Sing unto the Lord a new song; for he hath done marvelous things: his right hand, and his holy arm, hath gotten him the victory!" (Psalm 98:1).

Dare to play a different tune! The Word of God supplies you with the loveliest notes!

SEVEN REASONS WHY I PRAISE THE LORD BY SINGING

(1) Because the Lord hath put a song in my heart: "And he hath put a new song in my mouth, even praise unto our God: many shall see it, and fear, and shall trust in the Lord" (Psalm 40:3). Singing Christians are a tremendous influence to attract others for salvation!

(2) Because I am commanded to come before His presence with singing: "Serve the Lord with gladness: come before his presence with singing" (Psalm 100:2).

(3) Because God by continual repetition urges me to praise Him by singing: "Sing praises to God, sing praises: sing praises unto our King, sing praises" (Psalm 47:6).

(4) Because singing His praise so pleases God: "And at midnight Paul and Silas prayed, and sang praises unto God: and the prisoners heard them....and immediately all the doors were opened, and every one's bands were loosed" (Acts 16:25-26). In response to singing His praises, God often performs unusual miracles. He opens doors and He loosens bands of all kinds. By singing unto Him I discover a realm highly favorable to God!

(5) Because when I am filled with the Spirit, I

shall truly be filled with singing: "Be filled with the Spirit; speaking to yourselves in psalms and hymns and spiritual songs, singing and making melody in your heart to the Lord; giving thanks always for all things unto God and the Father in the name of our Lord Jesus Christ" (Ephesians 5:18-20).

(6) Because when I live by the indwelt Word, I shall possess spiritual songs: "Let the word of Christ dwell in you richly in all wisdom; teaching and admonishing one another in psalms and hymns and spiritual songs, singing with grace in your hearts to the Lord" (Colossians 3:16).

(7) In light of the strong commands to sing His praises, what shall I do? "I will sing unto the Lord, because he hath dealt bountifully with me" (Psalm 13:6).

Chapter 16

PRAISE THE LORD ANYHOW!

What about those times when the bottom drops out? When bills are overdue... When you've lost your job... Or lost a loved one... When your health is failing... When you're all alone? How do you practice boldly praising God when apparently there's nothing to praise Him for?

Well, in times such as these—and they come to all of us—praise the Lord anyhow!

Mr. L. P. Sabberd of Silver Springs, Maryland, shares this report: "Praising God under all circumstances and at all times is pleasing to Him. I learned this early in my Christian experience and have received many benefits from the practice of praising God even under adverse circumstances. One instance in particular happened a number of years ago when I was working as an automobile salesman. I had gone through a long sales slump during a period which should have been my best selling season. After several discouraging days of reverses, I called a customer about what I thought was a 'sure deal.' When she told me that she had already bought a car from one of my competitors, it was really a blow. But I got up from my desk and started praising the Lord right there on the salesroom floor. The joy of the Lord was restored to my soul, and I went on with the day's business.

"Despite a ten-day sales slump, I finished one of the greatest sales months of my career. Since then I have always tried to apply the praise principle to every circumstance—good or bad—and I just praise the Lord . . . anyhow!"

The sacrifice of praise has a vital place in the bold Christian life. It requires discipline. This is especially true because of man's natural tendency to be governed by feelings. When we do not feel like praising the Lord, then we must sacrifice praise unto Him. Feelings or no feelings, God demands a sacrifice of praise unto Him continually. "By him therefore let us offer the sacrifice of praise to God continually, that is, the fruit of our lips giving thanks to his name" (Hebrews 13:15).

We are commanded to "Rejoice in the Lord always" (Philippians 4:4), to offer the sacrifice of praise continually. We are not told to rejoice only when everything is going right, but when everything is going wrong as well. It is truly a "sacrifice of praise" when it costs to do it. When praise is most difficult, it is most necessary. Praise is the best way to sweeten the bitter and turn gloom to gladness.

My family—Joyce, Judy, Jeanne, Marisa and I—had been to Africa for several crusades. Our sons, Michael and Donnie, were serving the Lord in Indonesia.

The day came that our mission was completed. We left the Congo in the heart of darkest Africa to fly to

Paris. Because UTA Airlines was late in arrival at Paris, they made us their guests in a nice French hotel. We were given vouchers for transportation to Orly International Airport the next day.

Then the frustrations began:

1) Because we arrived at the Paris hotel very late at night and had to rise for an early morning departure, we only got three hours sleep. (As the events of the coming day proved, we could have stayed in bed and enjoyed a good night's rest!) 2) The hotel attendant drove us to the wrong airport—Charles de Gaulle International—dumped us and our baggage out and sped away. 3) We found a bus that could take us to Orly International, but the bus driver wouldn't honor the vouchers we had received the night before. 4) Seeing our predicament, we tried to make alternate flight plans and depart from Charles de Gaulle to New York City. Suddenly, heavy fog settled in and all flights from there were cancelled. Finally, an Air France official arranged for a bus to take us across Paris to Orly for a late afternoon departure.

Sleep had been lost, hours had been wasted sitting in an airport, we had missed our scheduled flights. We made a decision: we would "praise the Lord anyhow." Why be bitter at the hotel attendant or bus driver? Why chafe because of the fog and cancelled flights? We laughed our way across Paris. We laughed at the wild driving we witnessed on the freeway. We laughed with each other until the whole atmosphere of the bus was one of smiles on everyone's faces. It wasn't foolish laughter either. As Christians, we were reacting to frustrations by keeping our hearts light and rejoicing.

"Rejoice evermore. Pray without ceasing. In every

thing give thanks: for this is the will of God in Christ Jesus concerning you" (1 Thessalonians 5:16-18).

Don't miss God's best by praising Him only for those things which you label "blessings." His command is: "In *every* thing give thanks: for this is the will of God in Christ Jesus concerning you."

The sacrifice of praise unto God is a requirement of all Christians. Under the old covenant the Jews were required to offer animal sacrifices in order to obtain acceptance with God. But Jesus, the perfect Lamb of God, came to take away the sin of the world by the offering of Himself. No longer are we required to offer animal or blood sacrifices. However, God does demand a sacrifice of us in this dispensation of grace: the sacrifice of praise which requires sacrifice in self-discipline. And the results are glorious.

The people who lived in Ephesus during Paul's day, though heathen, sacrificed in praise to their false gods. We read in Acts 19:34: ". . . All with one voice about the space of two hours cried out, Great is Diana of the Ephesians." Diana was an idol, a false god of the Ephesians. If the barbarian people of Ephesus could stand and cry out for two hours, "Great is Diana of the Ephesians," how much more should we who know the living God devote ourselves to praising Him.

A converted atheist once told of the powerful effects of blasphemy. He said that he and other militant atheists were actually trained in how to blaspheme God effectively. Further, he said that the most proficient among the atheists could stand on the corner and blaspheme God for hours without repeating the same thing twice. As a result of this practice, they often became endued with strange and supernatural powers, he reported, and many startling signs and seeming miracles were wrought.

If militant atheists can blaspheme the living God for hours, how much more praise is due from our hearts and lips for our wonderful Lord? Have you ever praised God for hours without stopping? If you did, would not the genuine supernatural power of God possess you and work His true signs and miracles in your life?

In Old Testament days, 38,000 Levites were appointed to serve in spiritual ministry unto the Lord. Of that number, David appointed 4,000 to do nothing but praise the Lord, play instruments, and celebrate and recount His glories and victories.

You, too, can be a Levitic praiser today, one who blesses the Lord at all times, who offers the sacrifice of praise to God continually. Begin by praising the Lord for two minutes if you like; then extend the time until you become a skillful and joyful praiser of the Lord.

When you can't think of a thing to praise the Lord for, here are a few suggestions to get you started praising. After you've "primed the pump," as it were, it will be easy then to "forget not all his benefits" (Psalm 103:2).

Praise the Lord, first of all, for salvation.

> "But ye are a chosen generation, a royal priesthood, a holy nation, a peculiar people; that ye should show forth the praises of him who hath called you out of darkness into his marvelous light" (1 Peter 2:9).

> "... Rejoice, because your names are

written in heaven" (Luke 10:20).

"Behold, God is my salvation; I will trust, and not be afraid: for the Lord Jehovah is my strength and my song; he also is become my salvation. Therefore with joy shall ye draw water out of the wells of salvation. And in that day shall ye say, Praise the Lord, call upon his name, declare his doings among the people, make mention that his name is exalted. Sing unto the Lord; for he hath done excellent things..." *(Isaiah 12:2-5)*.

Praise God for His unspeakable gift, His Son, the Lord Jesus Christ. As you consider the wonder of God's great gift, you can only lift your voice and shout with Paul:

> "Thanks be unto God for his unspeakable gift" (2 Corinthians 9:15).

> "For God so loved the world, that he gave his only begotten Son, that whosoever believeth in him should not perish, but have everlasting life" (John 3:16).

Praise the Lord because Jesus is the free gift of God unto life everlasting. Since salvation through this wonderful Savior is a gift, praise Him for giving it to us.

Praise the Lord because "the Scripture cannot be broken" (John 10:35). You have based your whole life upon the foundation of His Word. It is your assurance for forgiveness of past sins... Your present relationship with Jesus Christ as an heir and joint-heir in the family of God... Your future expectation to live forever with the Lord. All this is based upon His immutable Word. When you contemplate the fact that His Word cannot be broken, you cannot help but praise Him!

Praise the Lord because you know God Himself "inhabits your praises" (Psalm 22:3). Yes, the Holy One of Israel lives in, dwells in, manifests Himself in your praises. When you draw nigh to Him in praise, He inhabits your whole being, your circumstances, your problems and needs.

Praise the Lord because God heals and delivers today.

> "And immediately he received his sight, and followed him, glorifying God: and all the people, when they saw it, gave praise unto God" (Luke 18:43).

> "And he (the lame man healed at the Gate Beautiful) leaping up stood, and walked, and entered with them into the temple, walking, and leaping, and praising God" (Acts 3:8).

Praise the Lord because the Word calls us to praise.

> "Great is the Lord, and greatly to be praised" (Psalm 48:1).

"My heart is fixed, O God, my heart is fixed: I will sing and give praise" (Psalm 57:7).

"Let the people praise thee, O God: let all the people praise thee" (Psalm 67:3).

"From the rising of the sun unto the going down of the same the Lord's name is to be praised" (Psalm 113:3).

"Let every thing that hath breath praise the Lord. Praise ye the Lord" (Psalm 150:6).

Praise the Lord because through Jesus Christ you possess all things.
"He that spared not his own Son, but delivered him up for us all, how shall he not with him also freely give us all things?" (Romans 8:32).

"According as his divine power hath given unto us all things that pertain unto life and godliness, through the knowledge of him that hath called us to glory and virtue" (2 Peter 1:3).

In this great drama of bold Bible living, it is God, the Giver—you, the receiver. Since the gracious Giver has bestowed upon you "all things that pertain unto life and godliness," respond by praising Him for it.
"Blessed be the God and Father of our Lord Jesus Christ, who hath blessed us with all

spiritual blessings in heavenly places in Christ" (Ephesians 1:3).

This scripture doesn't say that He *might* bless you, or that He *is able* to bless you, or even that *you hope* He will bless you. It plainly declares that He *has* blessed you. Let every earnest seeker for truth meditate upon this—that the Father has blessed us "with all spiritual blessings . . . in Christ." You are blessed with heaven's best. Since God has blessed you, then boldly praise and glorify Him for such unspeakable blessing.

Praise the Lord because He gives you the desires of your heart.

"Delight thyself also in the Lord; and he shall give thee the desires of thine heart" (Psalm 37:4).

Some have the attitude, "If only God would give me my heart's desires, then I would praise Him." But that is the divine order in reverse. Praise Him (or delight in Him), and then He will give you your heart's desires. The Lord was pleased with David because he praised the Lord "at all times." How we please the heart of God, and how we delight our own heart, through praise. Delight in the Lord brings our heart's desires.

Praise the Lord because He gives you an abundant life.

"I am come that they might have life, and that they might have it more abundantly" (John 10:10).

In Christ you have bold, abundant life because by His grace you are a twice-born person. No getting bored with life, because this bold abundant life in Christ spells Life with a capital "L!"

PRAISE IS THE KEY

Praise is the key to the manifestation of God's presence.
> "But thou art holy, O thou that inhabitest the praises of Israel" (Psalm 22:3).

Praise is the key to the revealed glory of God.
> "Whoso offereth praise glorifieth me..." (Psalm 50:23).

Praise is the key to doing God's will here on earth.
> "In every thing give thanks: for this is the will of God in Christ Jesus concerning you" (I Thessalonians 5:18).

Praise is the key to fulfilling the Father's desire for true worshippers.
> "Lift up your hands in the sanctuary, and bless the Lord" (Psalm 134:2).

Praise is the key to a fruit-bearing life.
> "...That is, the fruit of our lips, giving thanks to his name" (Hebrews 13:15).

> "Herein is my Father glorified, that ye bear much fruit..." (John 15:8).

Praise is the key to the Baptism of the Holy Spirit.
> "And they were continually in the temple, praising and blessing God" (Luke 24:53).

Praise is the key to the continual Spirit-filled life.
"And be not drunk with wine, wherein is excess; but be filled with the Spirit; speaking to yourselves in psalms and hymns and spiritual songs, singing and making melody in your heart to the Lord; giving thanks always for all things unto God and the Father in the name of our Lord Jesus Christ" (Ephesians 5:18-20).

Praise is the key to enter the very courts of God.
"Enter into his gates with thanksgiving, and into his courts with praise: be thankful unto him, and bless his name" (Psalm 100:4).

Praise is the key to respond to God's impartation of a song of praise in our hearts.
"And he hath put a new song in my mouth, even praise unto our God: many shall see it, and fear, and shall trust in the Lord" (Psalm 40:3).

I SEE I AM FREE...

Chapter 17

TO HIM WHO OVERCOMES

In my travels as an evangelist, I have found that multitudes of people are oppressed by worry, insomnia, nervousness, sexual impurities and many other disturbances. I have often stated that too many Christians are plagued by the "CDT'S." The "CDT'S" are "cares, difficulties and troubles." While the "CDT'S" may sound amusing, there's absolutely nothing amusing about the results they bring upon people's lives.

There are times when life is full of frustrations, and we seem to be plagued with problems. Yet Jesus, who is our strength in the midst of these times, gives us a very blessed promise to help in our bold Bible living against these negative situations. Jesus says, "He who *overcomes*, I will grant to him to sit down with Me on My throne, as I also overcame and sat down with My Father on His throne" (Revelation 3:21 *New American Standard*). What a marvelous promise! Jesus has actually promised us a seat with Him on His throne for all time if we will be overcomers.

I have received many letters over the years

concerning the areas people find most difficult to overcome. Perhaps the following questions and biblical answers will encourage you to overcome everything that hinders your progress in bold Bible living.

"Many times I have tried to forgive a certain person for a wrong done deliberately, but I simply cannot. Is it really necessary to forgive?"

I can certainly sympathize with your difficulties, for in my younger Christian life I had some real problems with forgiveness. Even today I know what it is to wrestle with this problem. As a minister of the Gospel, I receive some very bitter letters, and each time I do it gives me a jolt. But friend, for a Christian there is no other answer but to forgive.

I think that unforgiveness is such a serious matter that I call it the "cancer of the soul." In my travels I meet people all the time who have this type of "spiritual cancer."

We must always look to the Master, Jesus Christ, when we think of this subject or when we encounter someone who is so very hard to forgive. Consider the indignities, cruelties and barbarism of the trial and crucifixion of Jesus. Yet He prayed, "Father, forgive them."

I met a young man in eastern Canada who had been studying for the ministry. But he had been "double-crossed" by his employer. He became bitter. Soon after, another person wronged him. This only increased his spirit of resentment. An unforgiving spirit has now taken full possession of him. He has "cancer of the soul" and for the present has given up all plans for the ministry.

Jesus said that our reactions should be very different: "Love your enemies . . . and do good to them that hate you" (Matthew 5:44).

How many people allow their lives to be marred because they hold a grudge against someone? To learn how to be criticized and take it as a Christian is one of the most needed developments we can make in our Christian lives. Differences between people arise. But we must never let them give place to bitterness, malice, ill-will or resentment. Rather we should allow the love of Christ to flood our souls.

Actually, there is a higher cost to unforgiveness than most people imagine. Remember, Jesus said, "If ye forgive not men their trespasses, neither will your Father forgive your trespasses" (Matthew 6:15). What a terrible state to be in: to have the forgiveness of God withheld from us!

In Matthew, chapter eighteen, Jesus told a parable about a certain man who was forgiven a debt equal to ten million dollars. Then that same man went out and found a second man who owed him only twenty dollars. The first man would not forgive the second man that small debt but had him thrown into prison. When the king heard of the first man's lack of compassion and injustice, he had him cast to the tormentors.

Jesus then said to His disciples, "So likewise . . ." So likewise what? "So likewise shall my heavenly Father do also *unto you*, if ye from your hearts forgive not every one . . . their trespasses" (Matthew 18:35). Jesus cannot break His Word. Unforgiveness will result in being delivered to the tormentors!

What are the tormentors we will be delivered to? Anything that torments, such as nervousness, migraine headaches, ulcers, sleeplessness, fears, mental oppressions, unanswered prayers, bitterness of spirit, and the list goes on.

This is not a pleasant truth, but we cannot evade it. We *can* be delivered out of the hands of the tormentors. How? By practicing sincere and loving forgiveness towards those who have wronged us!

Whether those who have hurt you ask you to forgive them or not, Jesus said that from your heart you must forgive them. If you don't, you pay the price of being delivered to the tormentors.

Ask God to reveal to you those people against whom you have resentments. Whether they are dead or alive, you must forgive them. It is from the heart that forgiveness must be manifested. The Holy Spirit will do His office work by revealing those against whom you feel resentment because they have hurt you. Forgive them; then pray for them. Love them. God's grace will enable you to do it!

"I get so upset and discouraged because of the sexual temptations that I constantly have. I so want to be a pure Christian, but these temptations are strong."

First of all, remember this very imporatnt fact: It is not *temptation* that is sin—it is *yielding* to that temptation. Temptation comes to all Christians, but it only becomes sin when we yield to it. My first pastor, M. E. Ramey, used to say to us young Christians, "You cannot stop the birds from flying over your hair, but you can keep them from building their nests in it."

Remember also that "There hath no temptation

218

taken you but such as is common to man: but God is faithful, who will not suffer you to be tempted above that ye are able; but will with the temptation also make a way to escape, that ye may be able to bear it" (1 Corinthians 10:13). God has given His Word and He cannot lie: No temptation will come upon us that is beyond what we are able to bear.

Again, "Blessed is the man that endureth temptation: for when he is tried, he shall receive the crown of life, which the Lord hath promised to them that love him" (James 1:12). God will greatly bless those who endure and overcome temptation because of their love for the Lord and His commandments.

Of course, you must realize that sex itself is not a sin. It is a very beautiful function of the body that is given by God. However, the Bible very clearly defines the proper areas of sexual activity. It is only to be engaged in by married couples. "Marriage is honorable in all, and the bed undefiled: but whoremongers and adulterers God will judge" (Hebrews 13:4).

If you fear God and want to please Him, then you will not be careless along these lines but will wait for any sexual activity until after marriage. And you will confine that activity to your marriage partner alone.

I know of one young minister who demonstrated a great deal of bold Bible courage, not in what he did, but in what he did not do. I shall call this young man Steve.

Steve was a dynamic young pastor, about thirty years old and very successful in the pastorate. In his church of 250 members was a talented young woman who was very active in church work. It appeared that this young woman loved the Lord and wanted to please God by earnestly seeking him at the altar of prayer. However, she was married to a fellow whom she called a "spiritual dud." He was a Christian, but he didn't live on the same spiritual plane as his wife.

With time, this woman found her pastor "just right" spiritually; he was also quite attractive and personable.

One day Steve was invited to visit the couple at their home. Possibly prearranged by the wife, the husband was away when Steve called. He was informed of this only minutes after the young woman welcomed him at the door.

The woman promptly took advantage of the time alone with the pastor to explain her unhappiness with her husband. And then, in subtle ways, she began to compliment Steve. Being a man and sensing the danger of her attitude, Steve realized that he had to leave immediately. Before he could even get to the door, the young woman reached for his arm and stopped him.

Looking up into his eyes she appealed, "I need you very much; I want you very much; please take me."

The stage was set for the downfall of a godly man. Steve, however, walked away and won a mighty spiritual victory. Later, he told me this full account and the powerful temptations that seized him in those awful moments. It was no easy matter to walk away from that woman's door.

We drove far out into the country where he poured out his heart about the whole matter. "Brother Gossett," he cried, "I would rather die than commit adultery and bring shame to my Lord and my family!" I prayed with him and thanked the Lord for giving

Steve the courage to resist the woman's invitation. Thanks be to God, just as Joseph in times of old, Steve had full victory in his time of testing.

And you, too, can resist today's worldly cries for permissive sex and unclean passion and walk away victorious in Christ!

"I have been plagued all of my life with worrying and nervousness. Now that I am a Christian I want to be free. What should I do?"

There are many other people who are bothered by worrying and nervousness. Multitudes of people go through life needlessly worrying about everything. But worry can't help you... Worry never solved a problem, never paid a bill, never healed a sickness. Jesus said, "Which of you by taking thought (that is, anxious thought, care or worry) can add one cubit unto his stature?... Take no thought, saying, What shall we eat? or, What shall we drink? or, Wherewithal shall we be clothed?... for your heavenly Father knoweth that ye have need of all these things. But seek ye first the kingdom of God, and his righteousness; and all these things shall be added unto you" (Matthew 6:27, 31-33). Put the Lord first!

Then look at Psalm 55:22, "Cast thy burden upon the Lord, and he shall sustain thee: he shall never suffer the righteous to be moved."

What have you to worry about if you cast all your problems on Him? God has the answer to those problems, and He can work them out so easily. Put your trust in Jesus right now, and let all your worries roll on Him.

The same thing applies when you suffer nervousness. Nervousness is just an outgrowth of worry and the lack of trust in God. What a great plague this is to many lives. How people are driven into fretting and stewing over problems, persons or situations that may or may not be a real cause for anxiety.

Read the 91st Psalm, "He that dwelleth in the secret place of the Most High shall abide under the shadow of the Almighty. I will say of the Lord, He is my refuge and my fortress: my God; in him will I trust. . . . He shall cover thee with his feathers, and under his wings shall thou trust."

You won't be nervous and upset if you will learn how to dwell in God's secret place, under His wings. You ask, "How can I dwell there?" By reading His Word and by believing it! *God is in His Word.* When you put yourself into the shelter of His truth, He is there with you. I challenge you: look at His Word, read it, focus your attention on it, believe it, dwell in it, and victory over worry and nervousness will be yours—and much more besides!

"So often I feel left out and worthless. Do you think this is just self-pity?"

The devil is a specialist in his field of sowing seeds of self-pity in the minds of Christians. He focuses your attention upon disappointments you have experienced. Or he emphasizes your so-called lacks, weaknesses, failures, shortcomings and mistakes. He brainwashes you to believe that you are about the worst off of anybody.

A woman whose doctor has diagnosed a tumor in her stomach is convinced that "my tumor is the biggest and most severe of anyone."

A man I know feels sorry for himself because he is not as tall nor as attractive as his neighbor.

All of these feelings of self-pity are satanically induced. "We are not ignorant of his devices" (2 Corinthians 2:11).

The devil tells you that you are not blessed as much as some other Christian—but that is a lie of the old deceiver. Just how much are you blessed? God has an answer for that. He says in Ephesians 1:3 that you are "Blessed with all spiritual blessings in heavenly places in Christ." Absolutely, you are as much blessed as anyone else you know! In fact, you are the most blessed person you know for you are blessed with *every* spiritual blessing! How can you beat that? Begin now to regard your life as one highly favored of God, richly blessed of Him. God says so, so it is.

But you protest, "I don't feel especially blessed."

Feelings have nothing to do with this declaration of God's Word. Feelings or no feelings, God's Word says you are blessed, so you *are* blessed! "The just shall live by faith" (Romans 1:17).

Any time the devil grips you with feelings of self-pity, know that God has provided you with victory over the spirit of defeatism. "Thanks be unto God, which always causeth us to triumph in Christ" (2 Corinthians 2:14).

Pity thyself? No! Praise the Lord? Yes!

There is a divine ingredient in the power of praise that will expel the satanic device of self-pity and allow you to overcome it!

"I have a great problem of sleeping well at night. I have tried sleeping pills and different prescriptions,

223

but nothing seems to help me have a good night's sleep. I know how important one's sleep is, so I would like your counsel on this subject."

For all those who are troubled with insomnia and lay awake restless most of the night, there is good news! A sure cure for sleeplessness: "For he giveth his beloved sleep" (Psalm 127:2). God giveth His beloved sleep!

In millions of beds this nightly battle goes on. It's the power of God versus the power of Satan. If God is the giver of sleep—and He is—then Satan is the author of insomnia. Jesus revealed the nature of Satan: "The thief cometh not, but for to steal, and to kill, and to destroy: I am come that they might have life, and that they might have it more abundantly" (John 10:10).

Satan seeks to steal your sleep, thereby destroying your health, peace of mind and general well-being. Sleeplessness breeds nervous disorder, depression and all kinds of infirmities.

You can route Satan and sleeplessness like Jesus defeated the devil in the wilderness, by declaring, "Thus it is written." Take your sleep, not by counting sheep, but by boldly quoting God's wonderful Word! "For he giveth his beloved sleep!"

Psalm 4:8 gives a vital key to God's gift of sleep: "I will both lay me down in peace, and sleep: for thou, Lord, only makest me dwell in safety." Peace is a prerequisite for sleep. Before laying down to sleep, pray out of your heart and mind all anxieties, grudges, sins, failures and disappointments. God will give you a clean heart and a right spirit (Psalm 51:10).

Cleansing from God and casting all your cares upon Him will positively produce peace, and peace is essential for sound sleep. Practice kneeling beside your bed before retiring and commiting yourself into the hands of the Lord.

Dwell in your bed assured of safety and sleep, for the Lord is watching over you.

"I am one who easily loses my temper. Things happen that cause me to flare up readily, and not only does it irritate my own system, it also angers others. Can you help me overcome this bad temper?"

I remember one time years ago when I saw a famous preacher lose his temper and injure his influence upon an unsaved man who was interested in salvation. As Christians, we must be on guard, lest by a loss of temper we would bring dishonor to the Gospel. "He that is slow to anger is better than the mighty; and he that ruleth his spirit than he that taketh a city" (Proverbs 16:32).

God calls it a real virtue to be slow to anger. Some people pride themselves in their quick temper. But God says that if this is your spirit, you are a fool! "Be not hasty in thy spirit to be angry: for anger resteth in the bosom of fools" (Ecclesiastes 7:9). This is God's Word, that anger rests in the bosom of fools.

Now if this is your case, perhaps it is because you are not truly born again; you have not been regenerated. You can obtain salvation today by repenting from your sins and by believing the Lord Jesus Christ died on the cross for those sins and rose again that you might live eternally (Romans 10:9).

Or you may be born again but not baptized in the Holy Spirit. This too can be taken care of as you read God's Word and accept His promise for yourself

(Acts 2:38-39).

If you are already a Christian, don't attempt to justify your wrong spirit. Some people try to explain away their tempers by saying, "Oh, that's my Irish blood," or "That's the German in me," or "That's the Indian in me going on the warpath!" However, if we are new creatures in Christ, and we are walking in the Spirit, then old things are passed away and all things about us will become new.

The thirty-seventh Psalm has long been a favorite of mine. Verse eight of that Psalm gives this command, "Cease from anger, and forsake wrath: fret not thyself in any wise to do evil." God says, "Cease from anger." Put it away from your life. Let the Spirit of God cultivate the fruit of the Spirit in your heart to replace that anger. "But the fruit of the Spirit is love, joy, peace, . . . against such there is no law" (Galatians 5:22-23).

Boldly overcome your anger! "He that overcometh shall inherit all things; and I will be his God, and he shall be my son" (Revelation 21:7).

Chapter 18

SPIRITUAL VITAMINS

This message has been used of God to bless multitudes when I have preached it in our crusades. Guaranteed by God Himself to do exactly what they say, these vitamins will only be effective as you absorb them into your life. Then speak them boldly and act accordingly, and you will "see that you are free!"

FEEL DEFEATED?

Take Vitamin A—"ALWAYS causeth us to triumph in Christ" (2 Corinthians 2:14). Always, everyday, under all circumstances, God causes us to triumph through Christ. Linked with God, we are victors...not losers.

FEEL DISCOURAGED?

Take Vitamin B—"BLESSED" with all spiritual blessings in heavenly places in Christ" (Ephesians 1:3). Why should you feel discouraged when you know that you are blessed with every spiritual blessing in Christ? We are already blessed...He *hath blessed us!* Blessed in that we are new creatures in Christ (2

Corinthians 5:17), we are the redeemed of the Lord (Colossians 1:12-14), we are the righteousness of God in Christ (2 Corinthians 5:21), we are partakers of the nature of God (2 Peter 1:4).

FEEL TROUBLED?

Take Vitamin C—"CASTING all your care upon him, for he careth for you" (1 Peter 5:7). When you know that your God loves you so much that He invites you to cast all your cares upon Him, then your troubles become only His troubles. He promises to work all things out for your good and His glory.

FEEL DOWNCAST?

Take Vitamin D—"DELIGHT thyself also in the Lord; and he shall give thee the desires of thine heart" (Psalm 37:4). Some folks say, "If the Lord would give me the desires of my heart, I would surely praise and rejoice then!" But it is by delighting yourself in the Lord *first* that He will give you your heart's desires. Begin to delight yourself *right now* in the Lord!

FEEL ANXIOUS?

Take Vitamin E—"EVERYTHING by prayer...let your requests be made known unto God" (Philippians 4:6). How God desires to care for you! The complete verse here says, "Be anxious in nothing..." Whatever it is that makes you anxious, that's the very thing to pray about, to commit to God for His intervention. The result: Instead of anxiety, "The peace of God, which passeth all understanding, shall keep your hearts and minds through Christ

Jesus!" (Philippians 4:8). Hallelujah!

REMEMBERING FAILURES?

Take Vitamin F—"FORGETTING those things which are behind" (Philippians 3:13). Perhaps your memory is your worst enemy. You remember your failures, your mistakes, your disappointments... you are robbed of your initiative for the present and future. Be done with this folly! Forget those things of your former years! They are past and gone. God forgives and removes our sins and failings from us. Accept His forgiveness and be willing to forgive yourself! God's dealing with you is in the present, *now!*

HAVE THE BLUES?

Take Vitamin G—"GIVING thanks always for all things unto God" (Ephesians 5:20). When the blues come, reducing you to despondency, give thanks to God joyfully and boldly—the blues will depart every time.

FAITH WAVERING?

Take Vitamin H—"HOLD fast the profession of your faith without wavering; for he is faithful that promised" (Hebrews 10:23). According to James 1:6-7, if your faith wavers, you will receive absolutely nothing from the Lord. To have unwavering faith, simply hold fast your confession of God's Word without wavering. Recognize that doubt is of the devil, and you can defeat the devil by "thus saith the Lord."

FEEL INCAPABLE?

Take Vitamin I—"I can do all things through

Christ which strengtheneth me" (Philippians 4:13). The words "I can't" have a big part in the speech habits of many Christians. The "I can't" attitude locks out the power and ability of God and causes you to fail all the time. But through Christ you can do all things, whatsoever He wants done, for He is your strength.

FEEL WEAK?

Take Vitamin J—"JOY of the Lord is your strength" (Nehemiah 8:10). Joyful Christians are always strong Christians. A joyful church is a strong church. Jesus is the source of your joy (John 15:11). Allow Him to control your life, and you will be strong and vigorous. His Joy is your Strength!

FEEL YOURSELF SLIPPING?

Take Vitamin K—"KEPT by the power of God" (1 Peter 1:5). When temptation comes, take vitamin K...God's power is keeping you! When you feel yourself slipping, vitamin K positively will keep you!

BAD TEMPER?

Take Vitamin L—"LOVE is not easily provoked" (1 Corinthians 13:5). When you are genuinely controlled by the love of Jesus, your temper will not cause you anguish or blight the lives of others. Walk in love and you will have mastery over a bad temper that upsets so many things. Remember: "Love never faileth."

FEEL GLOOMY?

Take Vitamin M—"MY MOUTH shall show forth

thy praise" (Psalm 51:15). Praise and gloom cannot abide in the same house. Whenever I meet a gloomy Christian, I know he is one that does not praise the Lord. Like gas and water, praise and gloom just don't mix. Real praise to the Lord dispels gloom every time.

FEELING UNSURE?

Take Vitamin N—"NAME of the Lord is a strong tower: the righteous runneth into it, and is safe" (Proverbs 18:10). In these perilous days of the threat of war, shortages and crime, only the name of the Lord assures safety!

BOTHERED BY SATAN?

Take Vitamin O—"OVERCAME him (the devil) by the blood of the Lamb, and by the word of their testimony" (Revelation 12:11). Instead of Satan overcoming us, we overcome him by the power of Jesus' blood and the Word in our testimony.

TONGUE TROUBLE?

Take Vitamin P—"PRAISE shall continually be in my mouth" (Psalm 34:1). Most of our troubles have been tongue troubles. The cure for an unruly tongue is to train it to "Bless the Lord at all times: his praise shall *continually* be in my mouth."

FEEL DISTURBED?

Take Vitamin Q—"QUIETNESS shall be your strength" (Isaiah 30:15). God's quietness for our spirits displaces all disturbed attitudes and ministers abundant strength to our lives.

CIRCUMSTANCES BAD?

Take Vitamin R—"REJOICE in the Lord always: and again I say, Rejoice" (Philippians 4:4). In this "package of vitamins," you notice the frequent use of these uplifters and fortifiers called praise, thanksgiving and rejoicing. These attitudes are the "sure cure" for every spiritual infirmity you may possess. When you practice a positive praise life, you'll never suffer a nervous breakdown, nor will you ever land in a mental hospital. Rejoice in the Lord! When? *Always!* There is occasion to praise your wonderful Lord *always.*

DOUBTING THE WORD?

Take Vitamin S—"SCRIPTURE cannot be broken" (John 10:35). Satan is the author of doubt. But the Scriptures absolutely cannot be broken. Read also Isaiah 55:10-11. God's Word cannot be voided. When you are dealing with the Scriptures, know assuredly they cannot be broken.

BORED WITH LIFE?

Take Vitamin T—"THANKS be unto God for his unspeakable gift" (2 Corinthians 9:15). Many people write us who are bored with life. But as a Christian, you need never be bored with life when you consider the wonder of God's great gift to us, the Lord Jesus Christ. Christ spells life with a capital "L." Jesus offers Abundant Life, Abounding Grace, Unspeakable Joy and Peace That Passeth All Understanding.

DOWN IN THE DUMPS?

Take Vitamin U—"UPHELD by the right hand of God" (Isaiah 41:10). When you know that God is holding you up, you cannot really stay down. Thank God for His uplifting, resurrection power!

HINDRANCES IN THE WAY?

Take Vitamin V—"VIOLENT shall take it by force" (Matthew 11:12). In the Bible, almost every miracle has this characteristic . . . *violent faith.* What is this violent faith that *takes?* It is undenying, persistent, wholehearted faith . . . this is the kind that Bartimaeus had when "he cried all the more, 'Jesus, have mercy on me.'" The Canaanite mother of Mark 7:26 was violent in her faith and obtained deliverance for her daughter. Regardless of hindrances that stand in your way to complete victory—"press through!" The Lord is a rewarder of those who diligently seek Him (Hebrews 11:6).

FAINTHEARTED?

Take Vitamin W—"WORD was in my heart as a burning fire shut up in my bones" (Jeremiah 20:9). Jeremiah in this chapter stands as a shining example of those who become fainthearted and discouraged. He first cried out against God, "O Lord, thou hast deceived me." Then he complained, "I am in derision daily, everyone mocketh me." His decision was firm: he would not speak any more in the Lord's name; he was whipped through and through. But then the "big dose of Vitamin W" took its effect . . . he found that the Word produced a burning fire shut up in his bones, and he just couldn't keep quiet. If you are fainthearted, don't dare consult your feelings, your circumstances, or how things are going for you. Act on the Word only; *it reads the same everyday.*

FEEL TEMPTED?

Take Vitamin X—"EXERCISE thyself rather unto godliness" (1 Timothy 4:7). When Satan comes along with his temptations, you must not succumb to them. You can "Resist the devil, and he will flee from you" (James 4:7). Exercise godliness by standing on the Word and refusing the enemy's attacks.

STRUGGLING IN YOUR CHRISTIAN LIFE?

Take Vitamin Y—"YIELD yourselves unto God" (Romans 6:13). The Christian life is not a struggle. It is a life of yielding unto God. Here's the secret of daily victory: Yield yourself unto the Lord. This is the way to receive healing, the infilling of the Spirit . . . simply yield unto the Lord. The more quickly you yield all unto Him, the sooner you'll know His great blessings.

LAZY AND LACKING INITIATIVE?

Take Vitamin Z—"ZEALOUS of good works" (Titus 2:14). Filled with zeal and love for the Lord will fire your spirit with initiative. Be zealous! Be fervent in spirit!

Now you are equipped with the spiritual vitamins for bold Bible living. I challenge you to go forth and apply them to every area of your life. God's Word will work every time, under all conditions. God says, "Attend to my words; incline thine ear unto my sayings. Let them not depart from thine eyes; keep them in the midst of thine heart. For they are life unto those that find them, and health to all their flesh" (Proverbs 4:20-22).

Do not leave any stone unturned in your quest for

victorious Christian living! Put these bold steps into practice and learn to say for yourself, *I'm Sold On Being Bold!*